PUSH OFF FROM HERE

PUSH OFF
FROM HERE

NINE ESSENTIAL TRUTHS TO
GET YOU THROUGH SOBRIETY
(AND EVERYTHING ELSE)

LAURA McKOWEN

BALLANTINE BOOKS
NEW YORK

2024 Ballantine Books Trade Paperback Edition

Copyright © 2023 by Laura McKowen

Published in the United States by Ballantine Books, an imprint of Random House, a division of Penguin Random House LLC, New York.

BALLANTINE is a registered trademark and the colophon is a trademark of Penguin Random House LLC.

Originally published in hardcover in the United States by Ballantine Books, an imprint of Random House, a division of Penguin Random House LLC, in 2023.

The twelve questions on page 81 have been excerpted from material appearing on p. 36: Is A.A. for Me (aa.org), © copyright by A.A.W.S. Inc. and in the pamphlet, "Is A.A. for You?", and has been reprinted with permission of Alcoholics Anonymous World Services, Inc. ("A.A.W.S."). Permission to reprint this material does not mean that A.A.W.S. has reviewed the author's material, affiliation and/or endorses this publication.

A.A. is a program of recovery from alcoholism only—use of A.A. material in any non-A.A. context does not imply otherwise.

Library of Congress Cataloging-in-Publication Data
Names: McKowen, Laura, author.
Title: Push off from here: nine essential truths to get you through sobriety (and everything else) / Laura McKowen. Description: New York: Ballantine Books, 2023. | Includes index. Identifiers: LCCN 2022040146 (print) | LCCN 2022040147 (ebook) | ISBN 9780593498118 (trade paperback) | ISBN 9780593498101 (ebook) Subjects: LCSH: Alcoholics—Rehabilitation—United States. | Alcoholism—United States—Psychological aspects. Classification: LCC HV5292 .M35 2023 (print) | LCC HV5292 (ebook) | DDC 362.2920973—dc23/eng/20221107
LC record available at https://lccn.loc.gov/2022040146
LC ebook record available at https://lccn.loc.gov/2022040147

Printed in the United States of America on acid-free paper

randomhousebooks.com

2 4 6 8 9 7 5 3 1

Book design by Susan Turner

For all the noodles

CONTENTS

INTRODUCTION

IN 2016, I RECEIVED AN EMAIL FROM A WOMAN WHOSE SISTER WAS struggling with alcohol. The woman who wrote me had been going through the typical emotional meat grinder of loving someone caught in addiction: She was exhausted, heartbroken, frustrated, hopeful at times, and hopeless at others. Her sister had started pulling away and slipping into dark territory. She didn't know what to say, so she asked me: *What would you have wanted to hear?*

I was just shy of two years sober then. The woman contacted me because I'd been sharing my battle with addiction and fight to get sober on a blog, a podcast, and through social media. I had somehow, and barely, climbed out from the dark place her sister was in. I wrote her a long response and at the end of my letter, I told her that if all of my words were too much, she could just use a list, my list. I wrote the nine most important things I had needed to hear—from myself, from others, from what I understood to be God—when I was in the dark hell of my addiction. They were the things I still needed to hear daily in sobriety:

1. It is not your fault.
2. It is your responsibility.
3. It is unfair that this is your thing.
4. This is your thing.
5. This will never stop being your thing until you face it.
6. You can't do it alone.
7. Only you can do it.
8. I love you.
9. I will never stop reminding you of these things.

In the years that followed her letter, I found myself referring back to these nine things often—*It's not your fault / It is your responsibility / It's unfair that this is your thing / This is your thing; You can't do it alone / Only you can do it*—whenever I'd come up against something challenging: facing the massive debt I had accumulated, leaving my career in advertising and jumping into self-employment as a single mother, dealing with the trauma underneath my drinking, confronting the food and body issues that resurfaced in sobriety, and more. Whatever painful, hard thing came up, the nine things seemed to provide a touch-point of wisdom, guidance, and reassurance. I know it's odd to say my own words helped me, but it's true (and anyway, I feel like they came *through* me rather than from me, as is often the experience with writing). When I published my sobriety memoir, *We Are the Luckiest,* in January 2020, I knew the nine things would be the epigraph.

After *We Are the Luckiest* came out, I immediately began to hear from readers who found solace in the nine things. I received screenshots, shares on social media, emails and letters, and artwork people had created, explaining how helpful they were in not only addressing the specific challenge of getting sober, but, as I had found, in facing all kinds of other things, too, from divorce and infertility to eating disorders and chronic pain.

A PANDEMIC-SPURRED EVOLUTION

The COVID-19 pandemic hit a few months after *We Are the Luckiest* came out. I was in the middle of traveling around the United States promoting the book when lockdowns began. I canceled my plans and watched alongside the rest of the world as all our institutions shut down: schools, airports, churches, banks, restaurants. Each of these closures seemed more surreal than the last, but I was shocked when I saw an email from my local Alcoholics Anonymous chapter announcing they would be closing the building until further notice. I'd never seen this happen before—not for New England blizzards, holidays, public emergencies—never. Although I wasn't much involved with AA at that point, the availability and steadiness of meetings were still a comfort to me; any day of the week, there were multiple meetings available. It was a place I knew I could go, but also somewhere I could send others.

While I felt strong and supported in my own sobriety then,

I thought of all the people who were newly sober or struggling and depended on those meetings to stay sober; those who would understandably relapse given this crisis and would have no place to go; those who would no doubt start drinking more heavily under the pressure of lockdowns and find themselves suffering alone. Of course, it wasn't only my local chapter of AA that closed down—everything was closing, everywhere. AA has millions of members worldwide who rely on those meetings to keep them sober, and for most folks, like me, sobriety is a matter of life and death. These were parents and children and siblings and teachers and healthcare workers and grandparents and caretakers and folks whom other people depended on every day.

Because I'd already built a large community around sobriety through my writing in the years prior, I felt I could do something to help, at least until things returned to normal, which at that point we presumed would only be a matter of weeks. Without thinking about it too much, I decided one Saturday morning in mid-March to host a couple of free online sobriety support meetings over the weekend. I put together a simple sign-up page where people could register to be sent the Zoom information, announced it on social media, and broadcasted it to my newsletter list. I cobbled together a loose format based on what I'd liked best about AA meetings: an opening statement about intention, a discussion topic or speaker, and then time for individual shares from the people attending (about their challenges, wins, and whatever else might be on their mind that day as it related to sobriety) with some guidelines. I also added my own elements: meditation, reading poetry or passages from books, and occasional feedback and commentary on shares. On Saturday, March 14, I hosted the first meeting.

More than one hundred people showed up, and there was a palpable sense of relief that we could gather together, even if it was only virtually, and ground ourselves in a common purpose when everything else was terrifying and out of control.

Most miraculous to me in those first meetings was how varied the attendees were. There were people who'd never been to any kind of sobriety support meeting (because they'd never been part of AA or something similar), longtime AA members who were curious to try something different, people in long-term sobriety, and many who were still trying to get a start; there were sober-curious folks who were just starting to wonder about their drinking and people who had been sober for years but found themselves on shaky ground because of lockdowns. So many people who'd never before experienced community in their sobriety remarked that they were blown away that something like this was possible when they'd been going it alone for so long. I'd had a strong, solid sober circle for many years at that point, and I'd forgotten how impossible and lonely it was without one.

Before that first weekend of meetings ended, I created a schedule for the coming week. I hosted two meetings every day—one in the morning and one at night—thinking it would be a temporary thing until stay-at-home orders were lifted. I started asking folks I knew in the recovery community to speak at some of the meetings. As the days went on, the word spread, and we started to see 200, 300, 400 people show up at the meetings from as far away as Yemen, Singapore, and

Australia. Something special was happening and we all felt it. While the world was unraveling, the time together in these meetings made us feel connected, grounded, and useful.

As I approached the fifth week of running twice-daily meetings, COVID cases continued to climb and it became more and more clear that lockdowns were not temporary. While I didn't want to stop running the meetings, it was becoming more than I could handle alone while trying to navigate parenting, my new role as a sixth-grade homeschool teacher, working, and the rest of the pandemic. When I announced plans to discontinue the meetings at the end of April, I received hundreds of emails and messages asking if I could find a way to keep them going. After a few phone calls with family and friends and some quick deliberation, I decided to hire support and give it a shot.

In the last week of April 2020, my right-hand woman, Brooke, and I pulled together a team of meeting hosts and the infrastructure to launch The Luckiest Club (TLC). I decided the nine things would be the cornerstone of the community— a mission statement of sorts—and our closing reading at every meeting.

On the evening of May 4, my colleague Eric hosted the first official TLC meeting. When he read the nine things at the end, it felt like something essential had snapped into place. Quickly, they became the heartbeat of TLC's culture. Members have even developed a shorthand way of communicating them, like simply typing "#8" (*You are loved*) into a chat or saying "Number eight" in response to a share, to remind one another how supported we are.

While the statements themselves are intuitive enough,

over time it became clear there was a need for a deeper understanding of each point and how it could actually be applied
in one's life. *What does it mean to take responsibility? How is saying
"It's unfair that this is your thing" helpful? How do people actually find
a community so they don't have to do this alone?*

That's what this book is all about.

Push Off from Here is a deep dive into each of the nine things
and is intended to be a guide for anyone who is either facing
sobriety, or already on the path and in need of reminding and
encouragement.

For example, I needed to be reminded every day in early
sobriety that I couldn't do it alone. At first, that "it" was specific to not drinking: putting together another hour, another
day, another week, of physical sobriety. Over time, that "it"
extended into the broader context of living: learning to feel
my feelings without numbing, addressing dysfunctional patterns in relationships, forgiving myself for the past, getting
out of debt, making peace with my body, changing careers,
and so on. As someone who tends toward isolation and extreme self-reliance, the simple reminder that I can't do these
things alone (and that I don't have to) is something I forever
need to hear.

But I also needed, and still need, to hear the other eight
things! In this way, the nine things work as a system of thought,
with each "thing" in juxtaposition to another: *It's not your fault*
and *It is your responsibility; It's unfair that this is your thing* and *This
is your thing.* Like all essential truths, the nine things reveal the
true nature of life resides in paradox.

THE ORIGIN OF *PUSH OFF FROM HERE*

At my first AA meeting, in 2013, I shared that I'd recently left my four-year-old daughter, Alma, alone in a hotel room overnight because I was blackout drunk. In the meeting, I was sobbing, suffocated by shame, and in disbelief that my life had come to this.

Afterward, a woman walked up to me, placed her hands on my shoulders, looked me straight in the face, and said, "I have a daughter, too, and I get it, what you're feeling. But you need to know, you can push off from here. You can leave all that behind."

I thanked her, left the meeting, and never saw her again. But her words stuck.

My path to getting sober was a scraggly, messy, off-the-page kind of process. Less like a line graph and more like a nest of hair drawn by a toddler. Lots of stops and starts. Lots of believing I had it handled and then drinking again. Lots of wanting to be sober but also wanting to drink. I thought this messiness was a failure on my part—that it should be easier, or that I should be smarter, more capable, *better*. In this way, so much of the harsh self-criticism and self-blame that made drinking so attractive in the first place was keeping me stuck. It took awhile, but somewhere along the way, I realized I would never be able to hate myself into sobriety. I had to love myself there instead, with patience and kindness, and *push off from here* became a simple phrase that embodied those sentiments.

When I'd wake up hungover, despite my countless promises to stop drinking, I reminded myself I could *push off from here*.

When, for the first time in my adult life, I put together one, two, three weeks of sobriety and then fell again, instead of calling it all a total failure, I'd consider how many wins I'd had in those previously unimaginable sober days and that I could build on those wins and *push off from here*.

When it all felt hopeless—like there was simply too much damage, too much pain and shame and regret to face—I remembered that woman, another mother, who looked me in the eyes and told me there was another way. That I could *push off from here*.

But the words also communicated the necessity of eventually going all in, firmly and wholeheartedly. The phrase itself conjures images of a boat setting out from a harbor or a swimmer pushing off from the side of a pool. If the boat stays tied to the dock or the swimmer holds on to the edge of the pool . . . *nothing happens*. You can't cling to what you know and grow at the same time. Or as author Brené Brown says, "You can choose courage or you can choose comfort, but you can't choose both." Pushing off means actually *pushing off*.

Over the years, in my writing, on social media, and in conversation, I've offered the same words to countless others. As it turns out, *push off from here* is as sticky for other people as it was for me. We say it to one another in The Luckiest Club all the time. Drink again? *Push off from here*. Have a brutal parenting moment? *Push off from here*. Lose your shit at work? *Push off from here*.

Forget any of the nine things? *Push off from here*.

Set against the nine things, *push off from here* reminds us of the most basic instruction in sobriety and life: We can only ever apply any principle in this moment right now. We can only remember it's not our fault *right now;* we can only take responsibility *right now;* we can only reach out to someone else *right now;* we can only remember that we are loved *right now.* It's a continual reminder that *here* is always present, always available to us.

A BRIEF CULTURAL HISTORY OF ADDICTION RECOVERY AND THE IMPACT OF ALCOHOLICS ANONYMOUS

Before we go further, let's zoom out a bit and talk about how alcohol addiction and recovery have evolved over the years and how this book fits in.

Prior to the 1930s, alcoholism was largely seen as an incurable and lethal condition, a moral failing, and a sin. People who could afford to get professional help would work with a psychiatrist or go to a hospital where they'd get the "purge and puke" treatment of barbiturate and belladonna, or else be committed to a long-term treatment in an asylum. Those who didn't have resources would rely on churches and community organizations like the Salvation Army for support.

Dr. Bob Smith and Bill Wilson, both alcoholics, co-founded Alcoholics Anonymous in 1935 in Akron, Ohio, and built it upon a revolutionary assertion: Alcoholism was a result of an inexplicable allergy to alcohol, not sin. This allergy, if left untreated, manifested in a mental, physical, and spiritual disease that produced a form of insanity. They believed the alcoholic could be restored to sanity by working with other alcoholics and surrendering to a higher power, and that by doing these things one would have a spiritual awakening.

In 1939, in an effort to spread the word of Alcoholics Anonymous, Bill Wilson wrote *Alcoholics Anonymous: The Story of How More Than One Hundred Men Have Recovered from Alcoholism,* later known as "the Big Book" of Alcoholics Anonymous. Soon thereafter came the Twelve Steps, which summarized their program of rehabilitation. In 1950, AA members founded Hazelden Farm, a treatment center in Minneapolis, Minnesota. Today, it is estimated that there are more than two million AA members worldwide, and around two-thirds of addiction treatment facilities in America are still twelve-step focused.

In 1953, Narcotics Anonymous gained permission from AA to use their program in its own, and since then dozens of other twelve-step programs have emerged, including Cocaine Anonymous (CA), Gamblers Anonymous (GA), Overeaters Anonymous (OA), and Sex and Love Addicts Anonymous (SLAA), cementing the twelve steps as the predominant language and model of addiction recovery of any kind. Culturally, since the 1960s when *Days of Wine and Roses* starring Jack Lemmon (1962) portrayed AA meetings and programming as the path to recovery for alcoholics, Hollywood has consistently followed suit. *Clean and Sober* starring Michael Keaton (1988), *When a Man Loves a Woman* starring Meg Ryan and Andy Garcia (1994), *28 Days* starring Sandra Bullock (2000), *The Town* featuring Ben Affleck (2010), *Flight* starring Denzel Washington (2012), and *Rocketman,* Elton John's 2019 biopic, all portray AA meetings and language.

As a result of all these factors, the language, philosophy, and culture of Alcoholics Anonymous and the twelve steps have essentially defined recovery for the past ninety years. While there's no doubt the program has been beneficial for millions of people across the world, including myself—in large part because of the ubiquity of meetings, the strength of the fellowship, and the elegance and simplicity of the twelve steps—like all programs, AA has its limitations and short-comings. For instance, the program was founded by men, for men (women and people of color were not initially allowed), and the culture and language still reflect this. (There is still a chapter in the Big Book called "To Wives," which aims to tell the wives how to support their alcoholic husbands and includes passages like "*Try not to condemn your alcoholic husband no matter what he says or does. He is just another very sick, unreasonable person. Treat him, when you can, as though he has pneumonia. When he angers you, remember that he is very ill.*") Such antiquated, patriarchal language, a strong emphasis on God, a binary view of drinkers (you're either alcoholic or you're "normal"), and the insistence on a singular way to recover make AA challenging for many.

While other, more secular and inclusive programs have emerged over time, such as Women for Sobriety, SMART Recovery, LifeRing, and Moderation Management, nothing has come remotely close to having the same cultural and clinical impact as AA.

In the past decade, new programs and paradigms of thought have emerged. Movements like "Sober October," "Dry January," and "Sober Curious" have sparked widespread, accessible conversations around alcohol use, devoid of labels and stigma. Alcohol-free bars and experiences are cropping up in major cities across the United States and Europe, and the alcohol-free spirits and non-alcoholic beverage industries have exploded, as have sobriety-focused social media accounts and podcasts. Several books have offered alternative frameworks, such as *This Naked Mind* and *Quit Like a Woman*. The label "Alcohol Use Disorder" or AUD (the diagnostic term used in the *Diagnostic and Statistical Manual of Mental Disorders* (DSM) as of 2013 for someone with an alcohol problem) is now used more broadly, instead of the stigma-laden and anomalous "alcoholic" label. And major media outlets like *The New York Times*, the *Today* show, *The Atlantic, Good Morning America,* and *The Wall Street Journal* have started to talk about alcohol use as a "we" problem as opposed to a "them" problem, particularly around the issue of women and alcohol. We've even seen the "wine is good for your health" and other fetishized myths about the benefits of alcohol (narratives that were often developed and paid for by Big Alcohol) finally get debunked in mainstream media, and in 2018, *The Lancet* released a groundbreaking report titled "No Level of Alcohol Consumption Improves Health." Although these shifts haven't yet led to a decrease in alcohol consumption or addiction, to me, they're a signal of hope and positive development in our overall awareness and societal attitudes toward alcohol and addiction. At the very least, we're seeing a massive departure from the one-size-fits-all, male-dominated, anonymous culture to an integrated, inclusive, "sober out loud" one.

When I got sober in 2014, AA meetings saved my life. They gave me a place to go and they became my first sober community. I still hold the twelve steps in my heart and use them regularly as cornerstones of my recovery; they've been integral for me, along with hundreds of other people I know. *And*—for the reasons mentioned above and more, which I wrote about extensively in *We Are the Luckiest*—I've struggled with some of the cultural aspects of AA that I see as dogmatic, fear-based, patronizing, and outdated.

Push Off from Here is not a rebuttal of AA doctrines (or any other program), but an actionable framework that integrates its best teachings alongside insight I've gleaned from science, psychology, trauma studies, spirituality, and wisdom traditions, old and new. It positions addiction as what it actually is: a human condition. It positions you, the human reading these words, as someone deserving of compassionate healing, not dogmatic fixing. Although I bring in as much research as possible and have conducted interviews with more than forty experts to inform my views, this is not a clinical book, and I'm not a clinician (or a mental health professional, a scientist, or an academic researcher). What I am—in addition to being a mother, a daughter, a partner, a friend, and a woman in long-term recovery—is a writer. Which means I've got a slight obsession with observing life, scratching way below the surface, and telling the stories that help make sense of it all. And this space—addiction, sobriety, pain, and healing—is the ground I've been observing and mining for more than a decade.

CLARIFICATION OF TERMS

There are a host of words and phrases (for example, *sober, sobriety, recovery, emotional sobriety, abstinence, addiction, alcohol use disorder*) that get used interchangeably in our culture, and they have different intents and meanings, depending on the context or person using them. For clarity, I've given definitions below of what I mean when I use these terms throughout the book. These definitions represent my views only.

Labels—Alcoholic, addict. I don't use either of these words to describe myself because they feel punitive and limiting. In my view, addiction is an experience I had, but it's not who I am. Additionally, these labels are binary (you're either an addict/alcoholic or you're not), which isn't an accurate representation of how dependence, addiction, or substance use disorder (SUD) actually works. I do use them on occasion in the book for ease or when quoting someone else. I know that some people like and appreciate these labels for various reasons and that's great.

Physical Sobriety—Being abstinent from alcohol, or whatever substance(s) you are/were addicted to. For me, this also extends to any addictive, mind-altering substances that negatively impact my presence or well-being. "Addictive, mind-altering substances" is an intentionally vague classification that has to be personally defined by each individual. I don't believe one can, or should, define what sobriety means for anyone else. I have taken an antidepressant for twelve years and in no way view this in opposition to my recovery. I have also, as I discuss in chapter 9, had periods of using prescription sleeping medication and anti-anxiety medication, which turned out to be counterproductive for me (and thus I made adjustments with the help of professionals), but similarly don't conflict with my sobriety. I would not, for example, count that time as "unsober" time.

There's a large, growing body of research about the efficacy of psychedelics to treat PTSD, addiction, depression, and more. What was once anathema in most sobriety circles (the use of psychedelics) may turn out to be a scientifically proven, reliable treatment. There is a baseline agreement that physical sobriety means the absence of the addictive substance, but in my view, the details beyond that are for each person to determine.

The three questions I use to clarify whether a substance or process is problematic for me are:

1. Am I being dishonest or secretive about this in any way, either with myself or others?

2. Do I feel powerless (or even challenged) to stop despite negative consequences?

3. Am I continually using this substance to avoid or numb reality or my feelings?

If my answer to any of these questions is yes, it means I may be in problematic territory and need to address it by talking about it honestly with people I trust and, if necessary, get professional help from a therapist or doctor.

Trauma—The definition of trauma I use comes from world-renowned yoga teacher Seane Corn, who says trauma is defined as anything that exceeds our capacity to cope and leaves us feeling helpless, hopeless, out of control, and unable to respond. This is the most helpful definition to me because it doesn't name what situations qualify as traumatic but rather defines trauma by the lived experience of the individual. It's important to note that "helpless, hopeless, out of control, and unable to respond" is not the same as being uncomfortable or stressed out (although continued exposure to stress can sometimes result in trauma if we aren't able to emotionally process what has happened). Trauma is a very specific experience that alters a person's brain such that afterward, as renowned trauma researcher and author Bessel van der Kolk says, "the world is experienced with a different nervous system."

Additionally, trauma exists on a continuum that's impacted by a broad range of factors specific to each individual. While research has identified adverse experiences that are typically traumatic for children (as you'll learn in chapter 1), there are no hard-and-fast rules around what qualifies as traumatic and what does not. This is important as you consider your own experience.

Recovery—This refers to the process of healing what's *underneath* the addiction itself. Also sometimes called "emotional sobriety," this refers to the health of our relationships with others, ourselves, our spirituality, our bodies, our health, finances, work, culture, community, and so on. Physical sobriety and recovery are related (I discuss in chapter 5 that I believe full recovery requires eventual, sustained physical sobriety), but they are not mutually exclusive; it is quite possible to be physically sober for decades and still not be in recovery.

Moderation, Harm Reduction, Abstinence—While there are many people, books, and communities that support people who are looking to moderate their drinking, I (me, this book, The Luckiest Club) am not one of them. Perhaps it's because I fell into an acute level of addiction, and thus moderation was never going to be a viable option for me, but after years and years of painstaking work to moderate my drinking that resulted in failure after failure (for me and so many others), I simply can't conceive of a case where moderation is preferable to abstinence. The mental load required to plan, monitor, adjust, control, and otherwise *manage* the proper or "ideal" amount of alcohol intake is exhausting to even imagine. I searched for that elusive third door for years, and I believe I would have died trying. In the end, it was far more peaceful to accept it wasn't there.

More critically, though, what I've gained from sobriety completely eclipses any loss. To think I would forsake all the gifts that have come from giving up alcohol so that I could find a way to fit a few ounces of liquid into my body each week is laughable. I can't prove that moderation was scientifically impossible for me, but my inner knowing is crystal clear: I would never have touched a fraction of my own possibility if alcohol was still in my life. As Irish poet and philosopher John O'Donohue says, "The normal way never leads home."

That said, I am absolutely a proponent of harm reduction as a productive and viable way to move toward abstinence. As we'll learn, the factors that influence both one's probability of addiction and one's capacity to recover are both too complicated and too varied to insist on total abstinence as the only measure of success.

Emphasis on Day Count—AA and other programs, including TLC, emphasize sober time as a measure of progress, although to varying degrees. The way I see it, sober time isn't everything, but it's not nothing, either. It's not so much about the drinking (or using, or whatever) itself, as it is about, as Holly Whitaker says, "building a life [you] don't want, or need, to escape from." And what is meant by that is not out-side "stuff"—money, relationship status, career success, or having no problems or hassles—but our insides: the relation-ship we develop with ourselves and the people we care about; how we show up in the world; the baseline level of peace and gratitude in our hearts even when the world goes to hell.

So, it's something like this: distance from the harmful be-havior matters, on a physical level and a psychological one. It's one way to track the miraculous act of overcoming the otherworldly beast that is addiction, and in that sense each moment, day, week, month *deserves* to be celebrated. But I know for some, and for me in the beginning, it was too all-consuming and ultimately defeating to count days. Resetting my clock at a certain point would have caused me to stop try-ing, and so I decided I wouldn't do that, because I couldn't afford to stop trying. On the other hand, one must balance honesty, one's own integrity, and the corrosive nature of se-crets. Simply stated: Do what works for you, but be honest about it.

THE DIAMOND IN THE CENTER OF
YOUR CHEST AND "GOD"

Central to nearly all spiritual and wisdom traditions is a belief in an inherent goodness, or divinity, in each person's nature. Although the details differ, the central idea is that within each of us lives the seed of pure consciousness, or enlightenment, and that this part of us transcends all the earthly manifesta-tions of being human, like our behavior, personality, accomplishments, mistakes, addictions, and even our physical bodies. This part of us is not earned by good behavior, nor can it be destroyed by bad behavior—it is simply *there,* beneath and above all else—the pure, magnanimous essence of who we really are. In this sense, it can be thought of as the *truest* part of each of us. It is our wise, awakened self.

The Buddhists call this *Buddha-nature,* which refers to the already enlightened nature of all things or the part of all ordinary beings that is like the Buddha; in Hinduism, it is called *Atman,* a Sanskrit word that means the universal self, or soul, distinct from ego; in Judaism and Christianity it is sometimes referred to as *Divine Spirit,* and in some forms of philosophy and psychology it is thought of as the soul, or psyche, respectively. In some of these frameworks (such as Christianity and Buddhism), the "something" this refers to is typically religious in nature, like a god or a deity, and in others (psychology, philosophy), it is more secular.

Although I'd always been a seeker and considered myself to have a spiritual life, it wasn't until I was in the depths of my addiction and facing sobriety that the idea of a higher power or my true nature became experiential versus conceptual. Sometime in 2013, I was in my living room on a Sunday afternoon after Alma's dad had picked her up for the week. The realization that I could not blindly turn to alcohol to blunt the morass of loneliness and grief anymore—not that day, or ostensibly any other day in the future—took my breath away and pulled me to my knees. I instinctively placed my fingertips to my heart and began swaying gently back and forth. After a few breaths, I connected to something deep within me, beneath the constriction and pain. For some reason, I visualized it as a diamond. Connecting to it, I felt an expansion in my heart, and a feeling of peace washed over me. I knew somehow that this part of me—the diamond in the center of my chest—was, for lack of a better description, the *real* me. I knew it was truer than anything I had ever done, truer than the pain I was feeling in that moment, and truer than all the terrible stories I had about myself.

From that point forward, whenever I've found myself beyond the depths of what I can bear or understand, this image of the diamond in the center of my chest has sustained me. For me, it represents the truest part of me, something that cannot be changed or destroyed. But it also represents the place in me that is connected to, or in relationship with, a higher power of my own understanding.

By "higher power" I simply mean something that is bigger than me. Sometimes I refer to this as "God" for brevity's sake, but when I do, I'm not referencing any particular depiction of God as a being, human-faced or otherwise. I have also called it *the Universe, the Divine Spirit, and the Divine*, and to me they all mean the same thing. My experience of God, so far as I can explain it in words, is a relationship with an all-loving, all-accepting presence. It is everywhere and nowhere, visible and invisible, inside me and separate from me. I experience it in the ineffable mystery and magic of nature (especially the ocean), in intense physical exercise, in the eyes and touch of my partner, whenever I consider the fact of my daughter, while in the flow of creativity, when reading something beautiful, and in the company of people I love.

It doesn't matter to me whether you believe in a higher power or not, or what your spiritual or religious background is, if you have one. The nine things are secular. However, I want you to know what I mean when I use these words and refer to these concepts. Throughout the book, I refer to the diamond in the center of your chest, or in some cases, just "the diamond," but I also say things like "true nature" and "wise self," and they all refer to the same thing. Feel free to use my concept of the diamond in the center of your chest, or envision another image that works for you. As for a concept of a higher power or God, that is entirely up to you.

HOW TO USE THIS BOOK

My hope as you read these pages is that you find yourself in the nine things, and that they meet you where you are, wherever you are. Although the chapters follow the order of the nine things, beginning with number 1, *It is not your fault,* and ending with number 9, *We will never stop reminding you of these things,* it's important to think of the nine things as a system of thought, not linear steps. While each has its own lessons and meaning, they lose impact when they're separated from one another. For example, *It is not your fault* is infinitely more powerful when balanced against its equally true counterpoint, *It is your responsibility.*

In each chapter, I've given writing prompts and short exercises to make the ideas meaningful and actionable. The prompts and exercises are informed by best practices and research in psychology, philosophy, addiction, recovery, trauma, yoga philosophy, and spiritual traditions, but they should not be considered a replacement for professional help. They can be completed alone, with a partner, or in a mutual-support group. My hope is that this book becomes a living, breathing, ongoing meditation—a tangible record of your recovery process: messy, tested, real.

One of my favorite philosophies about learning comes from the Buddha. He believed no one should ever accept any idea as true, including his own, simply because of tradition, status of the teacher, or history; he believed the ultimate test was always one's own experience. What I've brought to these pages are the ideas I've tested against my own experience as a middle-class, heterosexual, cisgender, white American woman and mother, approaching forty-five years of life and a decade of recovery as of this writing. While I've made a sincere effort to bring forth a diverse set of voices to this book, it's still written through my voice and perspective, and I recognize the inherent limitations in that. Some of the ideas here may be relatable to you; no doubt, some will not. The bottom line is, you have full permission to test everything here against your own heart, mind, and body, and recognize that my life experience may be vastly different from yours. That is what recovery means, after all: you, returning to you.

Lastly, before we dive in, I want to say this: Sobriety has been, by every measure, the greatest singular gift of my life. I wouldn't be here and you wouldn't be reading these words had I not found a way, with the help of countless people, to live life without alcohol. I know sobriety—whatever your version of sobriety is—can be the greatest gift of your life, too, if

PUSH OFF FROM HERE

1

IT IS NOT YOUR FAULT.

IT'S 2013 AND I'M SITTING AT A TABLE ON THE ROSE KENNEDY Greenway in downtown Boston on a hot August morning, across from my friend Grant. He's a partner at the advertising agency I worked for before I started my current job as an account director at a different agency down the road, and one of the only two sober people I know in the world. I'd emailed him a few days earlier, when I woke up hungover again and scared. Grant suggested we meet for coffee.

As I stabbed at the ice in my coffee, I explained to him what had been happening. I told him about the DUI earlier that spring, about leaving my daughter alone in a hotel room overnight a couple of months later, which had forced me to go to my first twelve-step meeting, and how that still hadn't been enough to get me to stop. I told him I never knew what was going to happen when I drank anymore and that I was

afraid, really afraid, both that I had to stop and that I might
not be able to. He listened and nodded and smiled his warm-
as-sunshine smile. He said he knew exactly what it was like.
He told me some of his own stories from years back. He'd
been sober twenty years by then—an inconceivable thing.

After a while he looked at me and asked, "So, what're you
going to do, kiddo?"

I was struck by the casual, curious nature of his question,
as though he was asking me what I was going to have for lunch
later. *Why is he acting like I have options? What does he mean, "What
am I going to do?"*

"I mean, I have to get *sober,*" I said, confused.

He read me. He knew the dense knot of shame perma-
nently lodged in my throat, the self-loathing I carried everywhere and the effort it took to live this way, day after day.
He knew my answer came from a punishing, punitive place
inside me.

He paused and waited for me to look at him.

"Girl, I want you to know something. You're not bad,
you're *sick,* as in *not well right now.* And it's not your fault, not
any more than it would be your fault if you had cancer."

"Yeah, I know I know," I replied, waving my hand in the air.
I couldn't hear it. I didn't buy that this was a disease, if that's
what he meant. And if he meant something else, the intimation
that this was anything or anyone else's fault but my own was
ridiculous. *I drank and kept on drinking. I knew better. I lost control.*

"You deserve to heal. And it's going to take time. You need
to do whatever you need to do to give yourself that chance."

The idea that I deserved *healing* was preposterous to me. *Healing* is defined as the act or process of regaining health, getting well, mending. To me, the word suggests that one has sustained an injury outside of their control, that something has happened to them—an accident, the death of a loved one, an illness—such that the natural, responsible reaction is to allow for a period of repair. Healing, as a word and a concept, carries tones of empathy and compassion. I couldn't fathom feeling deserving of either of these things when it came to my drinking. Because I was the one who made the messes. I chose to drink, despite the mounting consequences. I lied to people I cared about, manipulated them, betrayed them. I didn't show up. I didn't keep my word. I kept moving the line of acceptability further and further out. I chose alcohol over the people I said were important to me—even my daughter. *I had done the injuring.*

No, I did not need "healing." I needed to *fix it*. I needed to suck it up, get a grip, and stop fucking drinking already. I wasn't helpless; I wasn't a child. I was a grown adult approaching forty years old. I had a graduate-level education, a career with a string of promotions and accomplishments. I had experience and skills, and I made important decisions at work and at home every day. I'd already been married and divorced. And principally, I was a woman and a mother, which meant I was supposed to *provide* the help and healing, not the other way around.

I had become an expert at pushing through and pressing on while appearing to be unfazed—a skill I began developing very young. When my parents divorced when I was six, I distinctly remember walking into my dad's small, sad, empty apartment for the first time and smelling the weight of his sadness everywhere, as if there'd been a gas leak. I decided right then that I would make everything okay by *being* okay. I'd smile and be cheery and never let on that anything about our new life was different or upsetting.

The trouble is, it worked.

I was praised for being "strong" and "resilient," and as a result, I dug in harder, pushing away anything that might communicate dissatisfaction or, God forbid, need. I grew to believe I could fix uncomfortable situations and feelings—that it was my *job* to fix them—and if I couldn't, it was a failure on my part. In essence, I came to believe other people's feelings and problems, especially my parents', were mine. *I came to believe the problem was me.*

At the time, sitting there with Grant, I had no idea the extent to which this belief had shaped my life. Later, as I became more aware, I started to see the way it bled into everything. It showed up in the way I overcompensated in all my relationships, the way I acted both needless and desperate with men, the way I fawned over people who were angry and abusive to try to win them over, the way I overworked, the way I tried to tame my appetites for food and love, and yes, yes, *yes*, the way I used alcohol to blot out the pain of perpetually abandoning myself in these ways.

Over the course of the year following my conversation with Grant, as I kept trying at sobriety, I clung tightly to this idea of self-blame, but I also kept listening and learning. In AA meetings, I listened to the stories of other people who had come before me, and to those who were walking alongside me, trying to get sober themselves. I noticed that the people who got sober and seemed healthy and at peace weren't in the business of endlessly beating themselves up. They were honest about their mistakes, but they didn't wear them as an identity. They had a lightness to them, but also a solidity—an unshakable center. Most of all, they had a sense of humor about it all. They just didn't take themselves all that seriously, even as they took life seriously. In this listening, and in conversations with other sober people, it started to occur to me that maybe I wasn't the absolute worst. Maybe I wasn't all that different from anyone else in the end, and maybe hating and berating myself wasn't going to be the way through this thing. I slowly started to see the difference between the people who got sober and seemed to be free, and those who stayed stuck in self-hatred and shame.

What I noticed was this: People who kept blaming, whether they put all the blame on themselves or on others (two sides of the same coin, as it were), didn't get better. Some pointed the finger out into the world: to blame their partner, their kids, their boss, their parents, their luck, their job, their history; and others pointed it inward, on themselves. But the sentiment was the same. What's more, they hated themselves and that hate showed up everywhere: in their pinched faces and apologetic hands, in their shoulders, curved around their hearts like a claw. They wore it in their aggression and anger. They wore it in their speech, in their rebuffs of kindness and goodwill, as if, when directed at them, it must be a mistake. Sometimes they wore it invisibly, underneath the shellacked performance of a "high-functioning" person, like me. It bled out in stuttering eye contact and hands shaking under the table. These people, for whatever reason, could not, or would not, move beyond the shackles of blame; they could not see themselves as anything but bad and broken. I could identify this because I was one of them.

What I saw in people who got better was that they found a third way. They didn't push away the dark parts of themselves, but they didn't overidentify with those things, either. Similarly, the goodness in them didn't hold outsized weight. As author Thomas Lloyd Qualls said in *Waking Up at Rembrandt's*, "Believing you are good is like believing in the half moon."

The people who got better seemed to accept the whole of themselves, like the moon. Sometimes the moon is fully visible in light. Most of the time, it is partially hidden in the darkness. But neither the illumination nor the darkness changes the shape of the moon itself. Believing it does is a delusion. The moon is the moon is the moon, no matter what part of it is illuminated. And the people who got better seemed to understand that they are who they are who they are, no matter what part of them is made visible in any given moment.

As much as I identified with the self-hatred and self-blame, a deeper part of me reached for this notion of fullness. Or perhaps it reached for me.

· ·

It is only after years of sobriety that I can see how misguided my notions of self-blame were—how much more complicated and complex life is than a singular point of cause from which all effect follows—and how naïve and oddly self-aggrandizing it was for me to believe that everything that happened around me, particularly the negative things, were a direct result of my actions and who I am as a person. Although I still struggle against this conditioning and bend toward self-criticism, when it comes to drinking, addiction, and the places it brought me, I am free from the weight of self-blame. I also don't believe I am broken, or bad.

In the pages that follow, I am going to share personal stories—some of my own, some about others—as well as the ideas and concepts that changed my perspective and brought me here. You do not have to fully grasp the idea that *it is not your fault* right now; I can't imagine that you would. But perhaps you can allow a tiny seed of possibility into your heart. That is a good start.

THE THING(S) BENEATH THE THING

After I had my daughter, Alma, I fell into horrific postpartum depression that manifested primarily as acute anxiety and insomnia. I couldn't eat. I couldn't sleep. It felt like my body was attached to jumper cables connected to a running car engine. I lost forty pounds in two months.

Before I was pregnant, I wasn't drinking every night, although I often had too much when I did. The weekend nights were nearly always a drunken haze, but I frequently took breaks during the week without thinking too much about it. Once Alma was born, though, wine quickly became a nightly ritual. I counted the hours until it was acceptable to pour that first glass, desperate for some relief from the anxiety. But for the first time since my first drink at fifteen, it seemed to have stopped working. Instead of smoothing out my nerves and slowing down my brain, the alcohol only wound me tighter;

it felt like I went straight from that first sip to the morning-after spiral of anxiety and jitters with no magical release in between. In stubborn disbelief and frantic need, I began to drink more, faster.

One night after I'd put Alma to bed, I found myself sitting on the floor of our bedroom after several glasses of wine, leaning against the bed, digging the uncoiled end of a paper clip into my thigh. Back and forth, I ripped into the skin, dragging small, angry red lines into my flesh. I realized what I was doing only when my husband, Jake, walked in and looked at me, scared and confused, sat down beside me, and took the paper clip out of my hand.

The next morning, he said, "Babe, I don't think you have a problem with alcohol like you're an alcoholic or something. I think you're just using it to self-medicate."

Although his words reflected our mutual naïveté at the time (addiction and using alcohol to self-medicate aren't separate worlds), the idea that I might be drinking to self-medicate pain had honestly never occurred to me before. We were barely out of our twenties then. Everyone we knew still thought of drinking, even heavily, as purely a fun and social thing. Overdoing it was a sign of living bigger and burning brighter; consequences like being too sick to work or function the day after, mystery injuries, and not being able to account for entire blocks of time weren't concerning, just fodder for good stories. I mean, yes, I knew alcohol had always eased whatever tension I felt in the moment: It helped turn the volume down in my body and mind after a stressful day; it made social situations less awkward; it blotted out the frequent ambivalence I had about my marriage; it made sex and feeling sexual possible;

it made life feel easier and smoother all around. But I never considered my drinking to be symptomatic of deeper levels of pain. I never saw it as a harmful coping mechanism, only a helpful one.

At that point in my life, I'd been to therapy only twice, and only for a few sessions each time—once in college when my bingeing had caused so much weight gain and self-hatred that I felt powerless, and another time before I'd become pregnant with Alma, when I was suffocating from shame because of the emotional affair I was having with a coworker and my seeming inability to end it. Both times, I'd scoffed at the idea of digging into my childhood as a source of insight into present problems. I didn't see the point, or how the past and present were related. I'd grown up with the religion of personal responsibility burned into my brain. Talking about what my parents may have done wrong sounded like victim-speak. And besides, I didn't see anything particularly interesting or upsetting about my childhood.

"Medicating what?" I asked my husband that morning.

"Your family situation, for starters," he said. "The shit you and your brother went through was not normal. *This is not normal!*" he said, waving his hands up at the ceiling, in the direction of my dad. We'd been living in the basement of his house for a couple of months.

Jake was referring to the entire history and dynamic of my family, but also to the specific series of events that had unfolded in the months prior. Right after I learned I was pregnant with Alma, my dad had convinced me to come work for him at a company he'd started in the recession. My brother had already sold his own business to go to work for him, and my dad made me the same promise he'd made him: that it was going to be huge, a once-in-a-lifetime opportunity. More money, more flexibility! The possibilities were endless, he said, if I was brave and smart enough to jump on it.

Soon after I started working for him, he began suggesting that Jake and I move to Denver. It would be easier work-wise, he said. He could be a part of his new granddaughter's life, and we could live with him while we sorted everything out, if we needed to. Jake and I were primed for the idea of a fresh start. We didn't say it out loud, but we both knew we were in over our heads, emotionally and financially. We pulled the trigger and made plans to move six weeks after Alma was born.

The week before we were set to move, on a work call with my dad and brother while Alma was taking a nap, my dad told me he wasn't quite sure why we were moving out there because I wouldn't have a job when I arrived. He informed me that I'd be paid for another month, but then that would be it. He said, "Jake should be working after you have the baby, anyway, not you."

So deep was my fear of looking stupid or weak to my dad (if I hadn't seen it coming that was my fault, I figured) that I replied, "Okay, makes sense," and the conversation moved on. When the call ended, I walked into the living room and presented the information to Jake as if the decision was something I'd had a part in making. "It's fine," I told him. "We'll figure it out."

This pattern with my dad, grandiose promises followed by a sharp about-face and then gaslighting, was one I'd experienced my entire life, but at the time I was still too attached to the fantasy of him as my savior to see it. Jake, as an outsider, was able to see it more clearly. It was this, among many other details, that he'd been referring to when he said, *This is not normal.*

. .

Years later, back in Boston, I struck up a conversation with a woman I met at a twelve-step meeting. She was also a mother, had been sober for many years, and in meetings I heard her talk about drinking when her kids were young. She'd done so many of the same unspeakable things I'd done: driving drunk with them in the car, drinking through bedtime rituals, forgetting or missing important dates, leaving them unattended. We went for coffee after the meeting and I told her about a morning a while back when Alma, three at the time, shook me awake on our living room couch one morning. I was fully clothed and every light in the house was on. Jake had been away that night. I was the only one there to take care of her. I'd passed out. It made me sick to say it out loud.

She looked at me, smiled, and said, "I understand. You think you're the only one? I did all that stuff, too. It's what happens. But that's not who you are."

"Then who am I?" I asked her.

"You're someone in a lot of pain."

. .

It's not surprising I rebuffed ideas like this. Only in the past twenty years have we begun to understand the strong connection between trauma, shame, and addiction, and only in the past ten or so have such discussions spread beyond academia and scientific communities, thanks to researchers and authors such as Bessel van der Kolk, Gabor Maté, and Brené Brown, to name a few.

Before I got sober, I saw addiction as an issue of self-control. Insofar as I thought about it at all (because it was never something I imagined I'd need to consider), I believed people who fell into it were simply weak and, not only that, that they *chose* to be weak. I believed they lacked the basic desire and willingness to choose what was best for them and the people around them. They just needed to *try harder*, and were I to be in their shoes, which I *wouldn't be*, I'd have no problem doing that.

When I started going to AA meetings, and in conversations with people like Grant, I began to hear a different narrative. I was told it wasn't all my fault, but the explanations as to why I'd become addicted were still murky and mysterious. I heard it was a disease, that I was probably born this way, that it wasn't anything of my own choosing, only a fact, like having green eyes. I remember one of the women in AA saying to me, "There's no why, honey, drinking is just what we *do*." Which, okay, that was all more helpful than believing I'd brought it on myself, but it still sounded obtuse.

It wasn't just me. Nowhere in the twelve steps or other AA texts—which, as I said in the introduction, have established and defined our broad cultural and clinical understanding of addiction in the United States—is there a mention of prior conditions and causes, such as trauma. While this isn't a criticism (the information we have now simply wasn't available at the time), it does highlight a critical gap in our understanding of what causes, and how we can heal from, addiction. An understanding that—unless you are part of a modern recovery community, have learned about trauma and its relationship to addiction, or have access to a therapist who's educated about these things—you will likely not encounter.

· ·

As I continued to cling to self-blame and rely on my own willpower and determination to stay sober, I kept hitting the same wall. It wasn't working. I could put together short periods of sobriety, but eventually I'd drink again, further fueling the cycle of shame.

A major lightbulb went off when I was told about something called the ACE study, a 1998 longitudinal study that examined the way adverse childhood experiences (ACE) are associated with later health problems, including substance abuse. When a friend suggested I take the quiz to determine my ACE score, or the number of adverse childhood experiences I'd had, I assumed my score would be zero. I thought qualifying experiences would be limited to acute neglect, physical or sexual abuse, extreme poverty, and such. While those things are on the list, I was shocked to discover other factors I'd have considered insignificant, like divorce, a parent who is depressed, and feeling unsafe at home. I ended up answering yes to six out of the ten questions, giving me an ACE score of 6. I then learned that individuals who have an ACE score of 4 or more have a *700 percent increased risk of substance use disorder* (formerly called *alcoholism*).

This was hard to ignore.

The study also revealed that childhood trauma is actually very common. Sixty-six percent of the seventeen thousand people in the study had an ACE score of one, and 87 percent had more than one. Compared with people who have zero ACEs, people with ACE scores are two to four times more likely to use alcohol or other drugs and to start using drugs at an earlier age. Lastly, it didn't matter what the ACEs were. An ACE score of 4 that includes divorce, physical abuse, an incarcerated family member, and a depressed family member has the same statistical health consequences as an ACE score of 4 that includes living with an alcoholic, verbal abuse, emotional neglect, and physical neglect. Simply stated: Trauma is trauma. No matter what form it takes, it plays an indisputable role in addiction.

Dr. Daniel Sumrok, the former director of the Center for Addiction Sciences at the University of Tennessee Health Science Center's College of Medicine, summarizes it perfectly: "Addiction shouldn't be called 'addiction.' It should be called 'ritualized compulsive comfort-seeking.' Ritualized compulsive comfort-seeking is a *normal* response to the adversity experienced in childhood, like bleeding is a normal response to being stabbed."

Maybe there was something to what my friend Grant had said about being sick and needing healing. Perhaps my husband had been right about my drinking as a form of self-medication. And maybe that woman at the coffee shop had spoken the truth: Perhaps, more than being someone who was *bad,* I was someone in a hell of a lot of pain doing the best she could do with the tools she had.

Perhaps that's what is true about your story, too.

Every story of addiction traces back to an origin of pain.

In the movie *Good Will Hunting*, the pinnacle scene is at the end, when Will Hunting (Matt Damon), the self-taught genius from South Boston who spent his childhood bouncing around foster homes, goes to say goodbye to Sean Maguire (Robin Williams). Sean, a therapist, has been tasked, via court order, to work with Will to try to help him get his life on track. Despite a few promising moments of connection throughout the film, it appears as though Sean's efforts will ultimately fail.

When Will arrives at Sean's office, Sean is holding Will's case file, which includes graphic photos of the abuse Will suffered.

Sean faces Will straight on and says, "About all this, son. All this bullshit. It's not your fault."

WILL: "Yeah, I know."
SEAN: "No. It's not your fault."
WILL: "*I know.*"
SEAN: "No, you don't. It's not your fault."

Sean repeats this seven times before Will finally hears him and breaks down. As he cries into Sean's shoulder, he says, "Oh God. Oh God, I'm so sorry."

It's a powerful moment because you can feel that all of Will's suffering stems from the single, subconscious belief that what happened to him as a child was his fault. But the real insight is in his apology. *He apologizes for being abused.*

This scene, as Hollywood as it is, perfectly illustrates the ongoing impact of trauma in one's life. Will's troubles didn't end when he grew old enough to cast out on his own and leave his abusive foster home; he carried it with him every day. It played out in his own displays of physical violence, sabotaging relationships, the denial of his gifts, and his inability to trust or attach to others.

The tendency for trauma victims to blame themselves is known in psychology as Internalized Blame of Self. It's a natural coping mechanism that helps people, especially children, survive adverse experiences when they have no other coping resources to draw from. A traumatic experience often feels life-threatening; there is an element of shock and horror that leaves the person feeling helpless. To regain control over their environment, the victim will often engage in self-blame and internalize the message "It was my fault." While this mechanism can aid survival in the short term, in the long term it often causes self-sabotaging behaviors, like the ones Will exhibits throughout the movie.

Ironically, the sabotaging behaviors often mimic the victim's original, traumatizing ones. Victims of abuse often become abusers. Children whose parents treat each other poorly often re-create those same dynamics in their own relationships. Lonely, neglected children will become lonely, neglectful adults, or else will become inexplicably attracted to them. And yes, children of alcoholics become alcoholics; addiction often spreads like wildfire through generations.

These things happen despite good intentions. M. Gerard Fromm, author of *Lost in Transmission: Studies in Trauma Across Generations,* writes, "What human beings cannot contain of their experience—what has been traumatically overwhelming, unbearable, unthinkable—falls out of social discourse, but very often on to and into the next generation."

In sobriety, I've met hundreds of people from all walks of life who, as children and even adults, solemnly swore not to become the dark side of their parents' or caretakers' personas, only to wake up one day and discover they'd become exactly that.

I had to go only as far as my bathroom mirror to see that this was true. As I approached my forties, my life seemed to be continually plagued by drama, chaos, and pain. I had blown up my marriage despite loving my husband, despite swearing that having lived through multiple divorces I would never get one myself; I had become a liar and a cheat; I neglected my daughter although I loved her fiercely; I worked incessantly, but never had enough money; I could not stop drinking and drugging and numbing and running, even as my life was falling apart. If these things happened in discrete episodes, they might be chalked up to life's typical ups and downs. But it was deeper than that. I wasn't simply going through bad times— I was starting to have a bad life.

This doesn't mean you must go back in your life and search for excesses of pain and trauma that aren't there. As I've discussed and will continue to reveal throughout the book, the causes and catalysts for addiction are complicated and many. Not everyone who experiences addiction has trauma, and not everyone who experiences trauma falls into addiction. But you can be sure, if there is unprocessed pain in your past—pain that still animates you today, either consciously or unconsciously—it will continue to poison your heart, your life, and the lives of those around you, until you become willing to examine and heal it.

Doing so is how we move from blame to responsibility. It is how we grow ourselves up.

> **QUESTIONS:**
>
> *What are my beliefs about addiction and people who get addicted? Where did I get these ideas?*
>
> *What is my reaction to learning about the relationship between trauma, pain, and addiction?*

THE MASS DELUSION OF ALCOHOL CULTURE

Most people who fall into addiction tend to blame themselves for it, but when it comes to alcohol, there is an X factor that makes it uniquely problematic: ***Alcohol is both the deadliest drug and the most socially acceptable one.*** Not to mention the most accessible.

Unlike illegal drugs such as cocaine or heroin, or prescription drugs such as painkillers and anti-anxiety medications, alcohol can be obtained by almost anyone, almost anywhere, and can be used openly and without question. While tobacco is legal, there is now a social stigma around using it in public, and there are many public places where it's not permitted— bars, restaurants, and airports, for example—whereas alcohol is a key draw in these places. And yet, alcohol is the *most harmful drug* (more harmful even than heroin and crack cocaine), and in the United States, alcohol is now the third-leading cause of preventable death. While marijuana is legal in many places now, there are both legal restrictions and social norms around its use. For example, it's not widely accepted to pass around a joint in front of kids at a party, whereas nobody thinks twice about guzzling booze.

Marketing drives, in large part, what is socially acceptable in our culture. Whether or not you *believe* you're susceptible to the influence of marketing, you are. Even if you don't see advertisements on television, Netflix, or in YouTube videos, hear them on the radio or while listening to podcasts, or see them physically when you pass through a city or town where businesses are operating, you are influenced by the culture around you every single day. For example, when your friend posts a picture of his dinner with colleagues at the new, hot restaurant, you're being sold the restaurant (and the company your friend works for, and the town where the restaurant is located, and many other things). When your coworker wears their favorite concert T-shirt to work, it's an advertisement for the band and, for your coworker, what it means culturally to be a fan of that band. When you go running and see your neighbor out walking their golden retriever, it's an advertisement for golden retrievers. When you wear a mask in public (I'm writing this in the midst of COVID), you're broadcasting a whole slew of cultural and political messages; the same goes for when you don't wear a mask.

Alcohol is marketed to us *everywhere* we go, whether through explicit advertising or through the ubiquity with which alcohol is consumed in our culture. And you're not likely to notice this phenomenon (what is familiar becomes invisible) unless you're consciously trying to stop drinking. Global spending on alcohol advertising is expected to reach $7.7 billion in 2023, and in the United States alone, alcohol beverage sales in 2020 reached over $222 billion. That's hundreds of billions of dollars' worth of product pumped into our daily lives, available at restaurants, grocery stores, sporting events, concerts, liquor stores, airplanes, airports, beach resorts, mountain resorts, workplaces, gas stations, convenience stores, yoga classes, gyms, and "wellness" centers. It's socially acceptable to have it in our homes, in most public places, and at every kind of get-together, from baby showers to funerals. While the marketing and the cultural ubiquity of alcohol doesn't force the stuff down our throats, it certainly normalizes it to the degree that it seems innocuous. The result? Rather than seeing alcohol as the powerful drug it is, we view it as a social accoutrement, liquid courage, truth serum, or—as one of my friends once called it—the duct tape of motherhood. It is the only drug we have to explain *not* using.

I once heard a famous clinical psychologist who had conducted his PhD dissertation on alcohol say that were it to become a new drug today, it would be banned; that there's no way it would be legalized considering how quickly it permeates the blood-brain barrier and the immediate effect it has on our body chemistry. More recently, mainstream media have started publishing articles based on new research conducted over the past decade that reverses the long-held narrative that moderate alcohol use doesn't negatively impact health, and in many cases, is even healthy, à la the "red wine is good for the heart" trope we've all heard for the past thirty years. Following the 2018 report in *The Lancet* that concluded there is no safe level of alcohol consumption, a follow-up report by the World Heart Federation released in February 2022 stated, "Based on recent evidence, it has been concluded that there is no safe level of alcohol consumption." The report goes on to say, "The alcohol industry has also perpetuated misleading information about the benefits of drinking alcohol. This interference by the alcohol industry closely reflects the universally vilified activities of tobacco companies. Portrayal of alcohol in print and electronic media as necessary for a vibrant social life has diverted attention from the harms of alcohol use."

While it will no doubt take time for societal and cultural attitudes around alcohol to significantly shift and integrate these kinds of messages (and a shift in perception alone won't resolve the underlying issues behind *why* we seek to distract, numb out, and disconnect from pain, or the sources of the pain themselves), I bring it up—I bring this entire argument up—because the collective cognitive dissonance and delusion we have around alcohol is so immense and so absurd that it is impossible to overstate the impact it has on people who end up struggling with it.

Directly and indirectly, what is transmitted to us, and what we transmit to one another when it comes to alcohol, is this: *It's normal. It's the answer. But if for some reason you can't handle it, then it's not the answer, but it's also not the problem. The problem is you.*

When I've discussed these ideas in social situations or posted them online, I always get pushback from people who refuse to blame behavior on marketing, social influence, or any outside causes or conditions. "I believe in personal responsibility," they say.

Well, I do, too.

I also know how much more complicated we are, and life is, than that. I've used "personal responsibility" language to

deny this complexity in other contexts, either out of igno-
rance, because I hadn't experienced the circumstances I was
judging myself, or out of defensiveness, because it's hard to
admit how vulnerable and impressionable we are. In my own
experience, yes, I chose to drink initially. But I could not fathom what that choice would lead to down the line, because that
message is not what's plastered and pictured and reinforced in
our culture. The messages we receive around alcohol are messages of fantasy and delusion.

I'm making this point now because it colors everything
that follows. Like the person who gets told time and time again
that their abuser is actually a good person, or that it's not actually abuse if there's no physical harm, the way alcohol is
socially accepted and celebrated is a form of gaslighting. It
leads us to believe that when someone struggles to control
their alcohol use, it is a failure of the individual, rather than
the *natural result of ingesting a highly addictive substance.*

It's not only that our ideas about alcohol are simply wrong;
it's that they stem from false axioms altogether.

If these perspectives belonged only to popular culture, that
would be one thing. But they pervade recovery programs, as
well as mental health and medical practices, too. From twelve-
step meetings to primary care visits to therapy couches, alcohol
and alcohol use is still discussed as a "them" sort of problem—
as in, the issue belongs only to people who might, unfortunately,
qualify as alcoholic in AA's quiz—whereas everyone else is
fine. But the reality is, alcohol-related problems exist on an
incredibly wide spectrum, ***as in a fourteen-million-people-
wide spectrum,*** which is the estimated number of people
who struggle with alcohol use disorder in the United States

in 2019. Of those fourteen million, only about 5 percent will get treatment. For women in the United States, alcohol use disorder increased by 83.7 percent between 2002 and 2013, alcohol-related cirrhosis rose 50 percent, and alcohol-related visits to the emergency room increased 70 percent between 2006 and 2014. Alcohol use kills nearly four thousand U.S. teens each year, which is more than all illegal drugs combined. These are not small case numbers—they are epidemic ones.

In twelve-step rooms, people who don't qualify as alcoholics are referred to as "normies," meaning *normal,* with a sort of enviable, "if only" vibe. I never had a doctor question my drinking, and more than once, I was told to *have a glass of wine to relax* when I mentioned my anxiety or not sleeping well. I have had hundreds, if not thousands, of people at this point relay similar experiences with their doctors. Identical conversations occur in therapy rooms. I don't believe this is a conscious failure of doctors or mental-health workers; I believe, among other contributing factors, they are simply part of the same widespread cultural delusion.

Illuminating these things doesn't change the fact of addiction; it doesn't heal the underlying trauma, systemic problems, or emotional pain often found underneath, either. But it does shine a light on the monster we've hidden in plain sight. My hope is that each time the scales drop from another person's eyes, we wake up to the reality of this monster a little bit more, and eventually undergo an entire cultural shift around our view of alcohol.

In the meantime, I want to relieve you, the person reading this, from the gaslighting effect of such widespread cultural delusion, misinformation, and social acceptance around alcohol. I want you to hear this: You are not the problem. *You are not broken—you are part of a broken paradigm.*

THE ILLUSION OF CHOICE

I have a friend, Sam, who brought his sons, ages six and nine at the time, into a bar one Saturday afternoon to play pool. He shared custody with their mother, his ex-wife, and on this weekend, the boys were with him. His drinking had been a major factor in the dissolution of their marriage, but that hadn't been enough for him to slow down. After a DUI and nearly losing his job, Sam seemed to have turned a corner. He'd started to attend support meetings and had committed, at minimum, to staying sober when his boys were with him. He was doing well with this.

That day, he had no intention of drinking. The boys wanted to play pool, and they all liked the wings and pizza at this place. Yet, my friend ordered a beer when he put in the order for the food. "It's like I was in a trance; like someone else ordered it for me." He drank the beer, and then one turned into two, and so on. Tragically, on the drive home, he crossed over the lane on the road near their house and when he swerved to miss an oncoming car, he lost control and flipped the car. One of his sons sustained lifelong, debilitating injuries.

Another friend of mine, Kelly, whose two daughters are similar ages to mine and played soccer together, called me while she was in treatment for the second time, sounding bright and full of hope. She said she couldn't wait to get home and see her girls; that she'd met so many wonderful people in treatment and felt loved and supported. The day she was released, instead of driving home, she drove two hours in the other direction and drank herself to death in her car.

These stories are never-ending. Across every race, class, sex, and age, these things happen every day.

At one time I would have heard these stories and thought indignantly, as many do, *What the hell is wrong with them? Just fucking stop.* Even well into my own problematic drinking, I would've said that. I grew up in the *Just Say No* and *War on Drugs* era, a massive political effort to crack down on drugs and crime, which, although successful by some measures, ultimately established and calcified the cultural view of addiction as criminal and a matter of basic education and choice, a character flaw that could be fixed with a simple no.

Despite the mounting consequences of my drinking over fifteen years—thousands of blackouts, waking up in countless strange places, the DUI—nothing had managed to pierce my illusion of self-control. It wasn't until I left Alma, then four years old, alone in a hotel room for an entire night at my brother's wedding because I was blacked out that the bell went off. It rang: *This thing has me.*

Leaving her was so clearly not a choice. In my right mind I would never, ever put her in danger. I knew how much I loved her. I loved her inexplicably and completely. I loved her like my friend Sam loved his boys, like Kelly loved her daughters.

So then, why? Why hadn't we chosen what we loved most in the world?

Because we couldn't. In those moments, we were not in charge anymore. We were addicted. Addiction was choosing.

. .

The word *addiction* is derived from a Latin term for "enslaved by" or "bound to." When someone becomes acutely addicted, they are literally *bound to* the behavior or substance to a degree that responding to cravings and avoiding withdrawal is experienced as a survival need, even above food and shelter. Despite the differences in medical opinion on whether addiction is a chronic brain disease or a learning disorder, all views conclude that a key characteristic of addiction is impairment to the essential decision-making centers in the brain. Brain-imaging studies from people with substance use disorders show decreased function in areas of the brain that are critical to judgment, decision making, learning and memory, and behavior control.

"A common misperception is that addiction is a choice or moral problem, and all you have to do is stop. But nothing could be further from the truth," says Dr. George Koob, director of NIH's National Institute on Alcohol Abuse and Alcoholism. "The brain actually changes with addiction, and it takes a good deal of work to get it back to its normal state."

Even in the 1930s, Alcoholics Anonymous referred to this as an "allergy to alcohol," also phrased as "the phenomenon of craving." It states, "We know that while the alcoholic keeps away from drink, as he may do for months or years, he reacts much like other men. We are equally positive that once he takes any alcohol whatever into his system, something happens, both in the bodily and mental sense, which makes it virtually impossible for him to stop."

At some point, yes, every person who experiences addiction originally chose to drink or take the drugs or have the sex or eat the food or whatever. But nobody chooses to become addicted. Nobody would.

QUESTIONS:

What is my reaction to the statement "It's not your fault"?

Do I believe I have control over my drinking? Is this belief helpful or harmful to me?

What would it mean if I didn't have control over my drinking?

BLAME IS A DEAD END

Beyond all the research, evidence, and stories I can offer, perhaps the most convincing argument there is for dropping the cross of self-blame is this: *It doesn't work. It simply doesn't work.*

I tried.

I tried and I tried and I tried to beat myself into submission by blaming myself harder and for more. Eight years into sobriety, I've seen countless others do it, too. And it simply doesn't work. Not for me, not for you, not for anyone.

In my research for this book, I interviewed dozens of the world's top psychologists and spiritual teachers. One of the most impactful interviews I did was with Timothy Hayes, an American clinical psychologist with more than forty years of experience. When I asked him what the most common hurdles to progress were among his clients, he pulled out an 8.5 × 11 sheet of paper. On it were ten "Bottom Line Observations" he'd compiled, summarizing the totality of his experience as a researcher, teacher, and clinician.

He pointed to the second item on the list:

> Blame is a luxury item; it does not lead to the productive or constructive resolution of a problem.

I asked him why this was true, why blame doesn't work.

He said that as long as people are in a blame story, they can't apply themselves in the here and now. While it's important to acknowledge our experiences and feelings and to be able to accurately associate cause and effect so that we can learn from the past, holding on to blame indefinitely keeps us stuck there, ruminating and inert.

The main reason blame stories are unhelpful is that they are polarizing and fixed. When we blame, we tend to put people and circumstances into binary categories of good vs. bad, right vs. wrong, in order to protect our egos and calm the anxiety of too much complexity. The problem is, in blame stories there is no room for change, growth, or solutions. For example, if we're solely to blame for our addiction, we're simply bad and wrong, the end. We're doomed and we don't need to look any further, so what's the point of trying? On the other hand, if we place all the blame on our parents or on our partner, for example, then we can label them "wrong" and we don't have to examine the complexity of their humanity, or how we might contribute to our own misery.

Psychologically speaking, this way of framing the world is termed "splitting." It's a defense mechanism that arises when we cannot reconcile the complexity of a situation and need to feel a sense of control or virtuosity. While it's typically associated with children and young adults when they're still trying to develop a healthy sense of self, it's not limited to them, of course; we see these toxic blame stories played out by our political leaders and media every day. These us-vs.-them narratives are seductive because they promise simple answers and feelings of superiority, but ultimately lead us nowhere but further down into darkness, despair, and disconnection.

When we are in the "either-or" blame place we cannot see, hear, or love each other, or think critically. It is an absolute dead end, 100 percent of the time. *Solutions* exist in the paradox, in the space of "both, and" not "either, or." It is in this way that I see addiction as one of the primary portals for collective healing. Those of us who have the willingness and opportunity to walk through the pain of it—to drop the elusive shackles of our simplistic blame stories and instead step into the complexity of responsibility—emerge with a deeper understanding of the human heart. We develop a capacity for compassion and forgiveness—the real kind, not the platitudes—because we've been to the basement of our own pain and know what's required for survival there. We can't afford resentment—not toward ourselves, nor each other—and so we have to find a way to love instead. Or, at the very least, to accept. When we gain these capacities individually, we're able to practice them more broadly: in our families, our communities, and beyond.

But first, I want to speak to your singular, exquisite heart. First, you need to know your life is so much more complex and layered than a blame story. There are things that made you and there are things that you made, but none of you or your life is so simple as to be explained by the facile concept of blame. We're here to pull apart and put to bed old, tired stories like this and replace them with new, useful ones—ones that will lead you toward healing, toward wholeness.

This is where we are headed.

2

IT IS YOUR RESPONSIBILITY.

IN MY EARLY TWENTIES, I WORKED IN THE MARKETING DEPART-
ment of a big insurance company in Boston. One afternoon,
I rushed back to my desk between meetings to grab a folder,
and the person who sat next to me took the opportunity to ask
me a question about a project we were working on together.
It wasn't a quick question, but instead of telling her I was late
for my meeting and would talk to her about it afterward, I
tried to answer, making myself more and more late. Then, I
forgot what I'd come back to my desk for in the first place, so
I let out a series of dramatic, exasperated sounds as I flung
papers and folders around, trying to remember. My fit was in-
terrupted by Jen, one of our designers. In her sweet, soft voice
she said, "Girl, it's like you've always got roller skates on." She
didn't even look up from her computer screen as she said it.
She just shook her head and kept on working, doing whatever

she'd been doing before I tore through our workspace like a tornado.

I sat through my next meeting red-cheeked and sweaty, slightly humiliated by what Jen said. She was right, it *did* feel like I was on roller skates all the time, but wasn't that how everyone felt? Stressed out, pulled in ten different directions at once, always a little behind and a little out of control? At the very least, wasn't this how everyone my age felt?

Ten years later, in my early thirties and now a new mom, I was lying on the floor of the bathroom at the advertising agency where I was an account director, having a panic attack. I was supposed to be making a big presentation to clients in our conference room down the hall, but excused myself when I suddenly couldn't breathe and my entire body began tingling like I'd been injected with ice water. When I got to the bathroom, I threw up violently, and as it became more and more impossible to breathe, I crawled on all fours out of the bathroom to signal for someone to help me. Next thing I knew I was being wheeled out of the office on a stretcher and put into an ambulance headed toward Boston Medical Center.

As I lay there in the hospital bed waiting for Jake to arrive, my breathing and heart rate returning to normal with the help of oxygen, an IV, and some Xanax, I remembered Jen's comment. The roller skates. It occurred to me that ten years later, I was still living the same way.

On both days, the one in my twenties at the insurance company, and the one in my thirties at the advertising agency, I was hungover. This wasn't all that strange for someone my age working in those environments, with so many happy hours, boozy client dinners, in-office bars, and beer carts wheeled around the office in the afternoons. Being hungover at work, even *very* hungover as I often was, wasn't exceptional or interesting—especially not in my early twenties—just one factor of many that made it easy for me to justify and ignore the warning signs as they accumulated. But over the course of those ten years, I'd gone from drinking a few nights a week to every night. I'd started to black out more often. As I got older and became a mother, I didn't phase out the office happy hours, binge drinking with my friends, or laughing about coming in to work still drunk. I had also started to drink alone: popping into the train station bar after work to down a couple before I rode home, drinking a bottle of wine by myself while doing the nighttime routine with Alma, draining the minibar in hotel rooms whenever I traveled. And as more and more parts of my life grew increasingly chaotic—my marriage, my friendships, my finances, my health—I still didn't see the connection between all that chaos and my drinking. I thought it was just life. *Wasn't life chaotic for everyone?*

Eh, no.

Life is messy, no doubt. There's so much we can't control, and we are all bound to feel, at times, like we're wearing roller skates. But what I'm talking about is different. I'm talking about the roller skates we wear that cause us, and those around us, all kinds of unnecessary chaos and suffering. Oftentimes, we don't even realize we're wearing them or that we have the choice to take them off. I knew my drinking wasn't always great, but I didn't see it as the primal force of chaos in my life—I definitely didn't see it as the fucking roller skates! Similarly, we don't often know how dysfunctional our tendency to people-please is in our relationships, or how our repressed anger toward our father impacts our capacity for intimacy, or how the unresolved trauma from our childhood makes us controlling and hard to be around, or how our low self-worth drives our workaholism. Roller skates can be sneaky and take many forms, but we all know what it feels like to have them on: wobbly, unstable, and like at any moment we could be on our ass. Again.

While perhaps silly, the roller-skates metaphor helps illuminate something key about responsibility: Become aware of how our behaviors and beliefs, conscious or unconscious, create chaos and suffering in our life (seeing the roller skates), and then develop the courage to change those behaviors and beliefs (taking the roller skates off) so we have greater ownership of our experience.

"Until we bring what is unconscious into consciousness it will direct our life and we will call it fate," Carl Jung purportedly said. Until we are willing to take a hard, honest look at the unconscious conditioning driving us, we will remain bewildered by our problems and feel powerless to change them. We'll find ourselves in the same toxic relationship dynamic, or working for another controlling, narcissistic boss, or sober from alcohol only to find ourselves addicted to porn, and say, "I can't believe this is happening *again!*" But when we start to become more aware of the role we play in creating our problems, we realize how much choice and power we have. Is this hard? *Yeah.* Humbling? *Very.*

But that's why responsibility is the hard, good news.

No one else is responsible for my experience? Ugh. *Hard.*

No one else is responsible for my experience? Ugh. *Good.*

Notice I'm saying *experience*, not life itself, and that's a key distinction. You are not responsible for life itself—you can't be, that's a ridiculous and harmful idea—but you are absolutely responsible for your *experience* at a certain point. In other words, you can't control much of what happens to you, but you are still responsible for how you choose to respond to what happens to you, as an adult. This means different things to different people at different times, but at a basic level it means becoming self-aware enough to realize the effect your thoughts and actions have on your life and the lives of those around you, and then being willing to change what you can control. This almost always requires questioning your (often subconscious) motivations, beliefs, and values; learning healthy ways to cope with discomfort; and developing a capacity for acceptance and forgiveness. Taking responsibility in this way can drastically improve your experience of life, but it doesn't give you control over life itself.

The concept of personal responsibility is a loaded one. While it's true that the choice to take responsibility for one's life must happen inside each person individually, the vast disparities in circumstances, resources, support, and the impact of the various systems we live in can't be denied, though they often are. When this happens, personal responsibility becomes an oversimplistic explainer for people who haven't achieved the same results or accomplishments as those with unearned privilege and power. This is one of the ways the "pull yourself up by your bootstraps" ethos we so love in the West fails people. And on the other extreme, we find a never-ending loop of finger-pointing and infantilization, where people (or certain groups of people) are perpetually victimized and deemed powerless and thus should not be expected to take any amount of ownership or responsibility. Both extremes fail us, in life and in recovery.

We need compassion *and* accountability.

Kindness *and* honesty.

Support *and* autonomy.

Space to breathe *and* resolute action.

The kind of responsibility I'm asking you to take is an inside job. It asks questions like: *Am I aware of how I'm contributing to my suffering and the suffering of those around me? Am I doing what I can to decrease that suffering? Am I willing to let go of what I cannot control, and change what I can? Am I living according to my own values? Do I feel a sense of freedom in my mind and heart? If not, what's the next step I can take to get there?*

In this chapter, I'm going to share stories of how I, and others, learned (and are still learning) what it is to take responsibility, and offer some guidance, including questions you should be asking yourself as you work through what's blocking you from taking responsibility in your own life.

THE TEN-THOUSAND-POUND PHONE

I didn't know the last time I drank alcohol would be the last time. I'd said *Never again* so many times before, and I couldn't stomach hearing it one more time. Instead, I promised myself the opposite: I swore to make no promises of forever. I realized I could only do the day right in front of me.

And so, that's what I did. But—and this was the big difference—I also didn't proceed into my tomorrows blindly.

I knew, based on over a year of experience trying at sobriety, that the first days wouldn't be too difficult; the fumes of humiliation and a hangover would keep drinking out of the question. But I also knew that sooner or later—whether it would happen in a few days, or a few weeks—the urgency I initially felt would recede. I'd start to feel better, physically and mentally, and the seriousness of what happened, and the reality of my history with alcohol, would begin to distort and blur. I'd start to withdraw from the people who could support me, slowly delay responding to texts and calls, and begin to replace real-life interaction with sober people with quit lit, podcasts, and Instagram posts. I'd skip a meeting here, a meeting there, because I was tired, or I had to go grocery shopping, or I didn't want to deal with lugging Alma to a meeting or figuring out childcare. I'd bury myself in work and mothering and convince myself I was taking care of my priorities; *so long as I wasn't drinking, what did it matter?*

Slowly, subconsciously, I'd slip into the well-worn grooves of self-reliance, rebellion, and over-functioning. I'd tell myself I could handle it, that I was, clearly, *handling it*. I'd feel clear and productive and inspired, convinced once again that I had this. I could get sober in the background and *get on with my life.*

But in the background, all the same anxiety, stress, loneliness, dishonesty, and cognitive dissonance would continue to grow invisibly, like a virus. Eventually, they'd grow too big. Eventually, despite myself, I would drink.

And that's exactly what almost happened, a few weeks after the last time I got drunk.

For the first week after my last drink, I went to a twelve-step meeting every day during lunch. I'd taken all kinds of other new steps, too: leaving work right at 5:00, even when I didn't have Alma, to avoid any talk of happy hour; removing all the wineglasses from my kitchen that I'd "kept around for guests"; taking a different path home from work so I didn't pass my usual liquor stores. I put a pause on trying to date anyone or even flirting with the idea, because that was a big trigger, and deleted the dating apps from my phone. I'd promised myself I'd get a new sponsor and raise my hand more in meetings instead of only listening, and I *had* raised my hand a few times, but I still hadn't gotten a new sponsor. I reasoned I had time for that—I'd ask around soon.

One night after work I picked Alma up from school and headed toward the grocery store for a few things we needed, plus something for dinner. It was getting late and we were both tired and hungry, so on the way there, I decided to skip the hassle and go sit somewhere to eat. I weighed the nearby options: Panera, Chipotle, Bertucci's. Although I felt a little apprehension in my gut when I thought of Bertucci's, because they served wine there—I'd sat through many dinners with Alma, drinking as much cheap warm red wine as I could while she ate her butter noodles or kids' pizza—I ignored it and told myself I was fine. *I wasn't going to drink, obviously.* Besides, we had Panera and Chipotle all the time, I reasoned, and I wanted to sit down and be waited on, to have a slower meal.

As we walked toward the entrance from the parking lot, I could feel myself starting to negotiate, but instead of turning around and heading somewhere else, I pushed through, telling myself it was nothing. As we were walking to our table, my phone rang: Mark, my friend from AA who lived close by. I sent him to voicemail. I looked at the menu and talked to Alma about what she wanted, growing increasingly distracted by the noise in my head. The waitress came over, brought us waters, and asked if we'd like anything else to drink. I ordered a Diet Coke for me and milk for Alma, but as the waitress walked away, I immediately regretted my choice. I wanted wine. *What?* I decided if I still wanted it when she came back, I'd order it. Right then, my phone lit up again: another sober friend, Tara, was calling. I sent her to voicemail.

What the hell. Were they watching me?

While we were waiting for our drinks, my phone pinged with a text message. My friend who lived in California, also sober. One word: Hi.

Then another message appeared, from Mark. Just tried u, wanna grab dinner?

Jesus Christ, I thought, and stuck my phone in my purse.

For the next couple of minutes, the same thoughts kept repeating in my head, over and over. *Nobody would know. It doesn't matter. You can start again tomorrow.*

I looked at Alma. Thought about everything that had happened in the past year. All the times I'd said *Fuck it,* like I wanted to do right now, after hearing those same thoughts. *Nobody would know. It doesn't matter. You can start again tomorrow.*

I realized it wasn't what I did when staying sober was easy that mattered most, but what I did when it was hard, like right now. I saw that even though the choice to not drink felt like chewing glass, I had a choice. I hadn't always had that choice, not in the earlier days of this fight, when I was still terribly physically addicted, but right now, in this moment, I did have a choice. I had support right there in my phone, if I was willing to use it.

The waitress arrived at the table and asked if we were ready to order. I told her someone was coming to meet us and we needed a few more minutes. I reached into my purse, picked up my phone, and called Mark. When he answered I told him where we were and asked if he could come join us. "Like, right now," I said.

"I'll be there in five," he said, and hung up.

. .

I chose to tell you this story first out of all the hundreds of stories I could tell you about responsibility because it's not about me muscling through on my own, clearheaded, doing all the right things and making all the right moves, because I'd finally made up my mind and decided to stay sober for good. I chose this story because it's messy and was a near miss. Because it illustrates how quickly the ground can drop out from underneath us, even when we've learned so much and have come so far, and how easily we can delude ourselves into thinking that we've got this, that we're *fine*.

I chose it because more often than not, the most responsible thing you can do is ask for help.

The most responsible thing you can do is ask for help.

Read that sentence again, write it down, put it on your forehead, tattoo it on your arm, whatever you need to do so you see it every day. Because if you're anything like me, this will conveniently slip out of your consciousnesses as soon as you turn the page. It doesn't jibe with the whole strength, willpower, bootstraps version of responsibility we're so steeped in, and thus it feels weak and wrong, like: *Shouldn't I be strong enough / old enough / capable enough to handle this by myself?*

I get how seductive that thinking is. I really do. But not only is it unhelpful, it will eventually kill us. At the very least, it will keep us disconnected, lonely, and alone. Where's the honor in that?

I don't know where you are in your life right now, whether you're only beginning to realize drinking may not be working for you, if you're deep in it and need to get sober, or if you've got a bunch of sober time under your belt already. But I'm guessing if you're reading this, you're stuck in some way. And I'd be willing to bet a lot of money that you're still trying to battle through on your own—that you're holding back 10, 50, even 80 percent of yourself from others—for fear of being seen fully. Maybe you're afraid. Most likely, you're ashamed. Perhaps you're not sure sobriety is what you really want. I understand all of those things.

No matter where you are, I offer you this: It takes a hell of a lot more bravery and strength to ask for help than it does to keep pretending like you don't need it.

When you hear *It is your responsibility,* my guess is that part of you feels as though you're not strong enough to bear it. And what I'm telling you here is that you're right. You're *not* strong enough, but not because you're weak, dumb, or broken. You're not strong enough to bear it on your own—not sobriety, not life—because *none of us are.*

Over the years in recovery, I've had so many friends and family members tell me they're envious of the kind of support I have in the sober community. That they wish they had something like that. This tells me that as much as we want to believe in our individual strength, we desire connection *more*. We want to be seen *more*.

If this feels true to you, pick up what we in recovery circles jokingly call "the Ten-Thousand-Pound Phone" and start asking for help. Not later today, not tomorrow, *now*. It may be the ultimate act of responsibility.

SNEAKY BLAME STORIES

One Sunday, not too long ago, I went to meet my friend Jim for breakfast. I got to the table first and was looking at the menu when I heard the restaurant door jingle, and in walks Jim, dressed in all black, looking like some kind of giant ninja, with a huge, stupid smile plastered across his face. As he walked over to the table, I noticed he was limping.

"What happened to you?" I asked, knowing the answer.

"Jiujitsu," he said, groaning as he sat down, but still smiling ear to ear.

A few years ago, at the age of forty-seven, Jim took up jiujitsu. He is, as he says, the least athletic person in the world. Despite being tall and imposing, he was never an athlete, never threw a ball, never played a single sport in childhood. The only heavy-ish thing he's ever picked up consistently is his guitar.

"You look happy for being hurt," I said and smiled.

"I fucking love it so much, Laura."

I knew this was true because he told me the same thing nearly every time we talked, but it was fun to see him light up about it again.

He asked me how my writing was going, and I skipped past answering and asked him a question instead. "Hey, when you were at your heaviest weight, did you ever blame anyone else for where you were?" I can ask him this because we've shared the darkest parts of our stories with each other. Despite the details being different, our sobriety stories are similar (they almost always are). We were both using something outside of us to medicate what we couldn't feel, or face—he used food, I used alcohol. At his heaviest, Jim weighed over four hundred pounds. That alone isn't interesting, except for the fact that I knew he was miserable and felt trapped, both in his body and his life.

"Oh yeah, totally," he said without even thinking. "I blamed Beth." Beth is his ex-wife.

"For the weight?"

"For everything,"

When I met Jim, he'd already lost two hundred pounds, had become a life coach, and had divorced Beth. When he showed me old photos and explained to me what his old life was like, I couldn't picture it because the Jim I knew felt so different about himself and his life.

"Say more," I said.

As we sat there eating omelets and home fries, Jim told me how the constant refrain in his head during those years was *If you'd only . . .*

"I'd say it to myself about my wife, and sometimes *to* her.

"If she'd only walk with me . . ."

"If she'd only eat healthy with me . . ."

"If she'd only put less pressure on me . . ."

"I had a never-ending list of things I needed her to be so

that I could get healthier. Basically, what I was saying was 'If she could only do the hard work for me so I don't have to do it myself . . .' I was using her as an excuse."

"So, what changed?"

Jim recounted how, one day, he was walking alone through the town where they lived, feeling desperate and exhausted from fighting this same battle for so long. He said an exasperated, angry prayer to God. He said, "Tell me, why do I know what to do but don't do it?" He says he looked at his reflection in a storefront window and heard back, clear as day, this response: *Because you're a slave to your feelings.*

This stopped him. "I realized in that moment that I had a choice," he tells me. "All these things I'd given up to Beth, to this person—all this power, all my decisions, all my sovereignty—it came rushing back to me."

A couple weeks later, after a gig one night, he made a commitment to a friend. He told her that within the next nine months, he was going to lose one hundred pounds and be on his way to completing his life-coaching certification.

Nine months later, he'd lost 115 pounds and was close to finalizing his certification.

"Why nine months?" I asked him.

"I figured that's what it takes to create a new life."

. .

My friend Lisa has a similar story. When she got sober, she and her husband quickly realized they needed to get divorced.

"I intuitively knew that my drinking was my responsibility; I didn't blame anyone else for that," she said. "But I blamed my ex-husband for literally everything else. I thought he was the cause of all my anger and unhappiness. I thought, *If he wasn't such an asshole, I wouldn't be so unhappy.*" They fought over the kids, over the furniture, over the past, over everything. "I was addicted to fighting with that man," she says. "And it was exactly the same cycle as drinking. Once I started, I couldn't stop. I became physically ill. It kept me from doing important things in my life, and I'd need days to recover."

Similar to Jim, Lisa had a realization that she had no control over what her ex-husband did or said—that she never did, and never would. She realized she was using him to convince herself she was powerless because that was a lot easier than looking in the mirror. As long as she stayed in the cycle of drama with him, she didn't have to face the reality of her choices or admit that she *had* choices.

. .

I was painfully familiar with this line of thinking. One day in my second year of sobriety, I was brought home in a police cruiser (with Alma, no less) for driving with a suspended license and registration. The practical reason I'd been driving was because I needed to get groceries, and I was waiting to get my license and registration renewed until all my parking tickets had been paid off, which meant I had to wait until I got paid the following week. I didn't have the money to pay them off because although I made a decent salary, I was still living paycheck to paycheck, and all my credit cards were maxed.

The bigger reason I was in that situation was because I was completely irresponsible with money and had been my entire adult life. I had always, no matter how much money I made, *barely* kept my head above water.

When we got home, Alma went into her room and I sat on the living room couch staring out the window wondering what the hell to do next. The police car ride had been awful. Alma kept asking what was happening, and I had no good answer. And now, we were stuck at our apartment with no groceries, no car to get anywhere, and no money to fix it until I got paid. The mess felt too big—far too big for me to sort out. I started to slide down my familiar mental grooves of off-loading blame onto someone or something else so I could feel less ashamed. *My dad should have been better with money. I shouldn't have been stuck with all those student loans. My husband shouldn't have convinced me to buy a condo we couldn't afford, one that we'd eventually have to foreclose on. I shouldn't have loaned money to this person or that person.* On and on. And when there was no one else to blame, I started to rail on myself. *Why couldn't I get my shit together? What nearly-forty-year-old adult gets late fees for overdrawing their checking account every two weeks and has no savings?* My mind ran through all the embarrassing situations I got myself into on a regular basis: having the electricity shut off, getting my phone turned off, having credit cards declined at work dinners, not being able to afford trips home to see my family, still having to ask my dad to borrow money for my car payment. As my mind kept spiraling down the endless list of fuckups, I sank deeper and deeper into despair.

This felt like a new bottom. A new low. I couldn't even blame the drinking anymore.

Right then, I looked at my kitchen counter and saw the gi-ant stack of mail I always kept there, unopened. I realized that sitting there trying to figure out whom to blame for this mess wasn't going to get me any closer to a solution. But I could do one small thing: I could open the stack of mail.

I pulled up a stool and sat there, opening up each piece of mail, until I was done. At first, I felt like throwing up. There were mostly bills, some of them months late. There were urgent notices. Notices of cancellation. Collection notices. I made myself write down each balance on a piece of paper.

Even though I knew I had "a lot of debt," I had no idea exactly how much. As I kept opening the bills and recording the balances, I felt better and worse at the same time. I hated what I saw, but it felt good to look at it straight on, to stop pretending it wasn't happening. Just like with drinking.

After I finished opening the bills, I went online and looked up all the other accounts I had: student loans, past-due credit cards, random collection notices, and all those parking tickets.

After I was done, I grabbed my calculator, punched in every single line, and for the first time in my life calculated the total sum of my debt.

Over $100,000.

I stared at the number in stunned silence for a while, then went back over to the couch and looked back out on the street. People were driving by in their cars, to and from work or to the grocery store or to pick up their kids or to visit someone. At some point, the room had started to get darker—the sun was going down—and the way the sun was positioned created a reflection on my television screen. I could see myself in it, curled up on the couch. I felt so small, like a little girl. I even thought I looked like a little girl for a moment. I wanted to hide, to crawl up into someone's arms, to call someone and ask them to make it go away—to fix it. I felt sorry for myself. *Hadn't I gone through my hell already? Hadn't getting sober been enough?* I was trying so goddamn hard to put my life back together— had made it two years sober already—and I hadn't done everything perfectly, but I was a safe place for my daughter. I got promoted at work. I was doing what I thought I was supposed to do. *How was I now sober but without a car? Without a way to take Alma to school, or to get myself to the train to get to work, or to get us groceries?*

Looking at my reflection, I realized I *wanted* to see myself as a child. Because kids have the right to be taken care of. Kids aren't expected to be able to pay bills, balance checkbooks, stay on top of things like licenses and registrations and inspections. Kids didn't have to find their way out of one hundred thousand dollars in debt. Kids are supposed to be somewhat helpless.

But I wasn't actually helpless, was I? I was in a really shitty spot, yes, but I wasn't helpless. So why did I want to be?

It hit me like an anvil to the chest: I was waiting for someone to save me.

All this time, all my adult life, I had relinquished some or all of my power to someone else, usually a man—my dad, my ex-husband, bosses—people who I figured knew better and would guide me, take the reins, watch over me. I was a nearly-forty-year-old who may as well have still been nine, looking up at my dad, waiting for him to fix everything that hurt. To fix me.

I had all kinds of solid reasons to be this way, I thought. Perfectly understandable reasons that I could justify in therapy for years. Reasons anyone would empathize with. But that wasn't going to help me out of it, was it? Knowing the reasons why I was here and wallowing in my self-pity, however justified, wasn't going to get my license back, my registration renewed, my inspection done. It wasn't going to get my bills paid on time and make sure I didn't spend more than I made every month, and it wasn't going to chip away at that number over there on the piece of paper.

My history was valid, as was Jim's, as was Lisa's. We all had plenty of very real hardships in the past. Some of us have it harder than others—oppression, discrimination, physical disabilities, disease, war, poverty—and sometimes our circumstances can be truly insurmountable. But the most debilitating thing happening in my life right then was the belief that *someone else* had all the answers. That *someone else* could live my life for me, better than I could.

I realized that day on the couch—like Jim did on his walk, like Lisa did after her most recent argument with her ex-husband—that I had been choosing to believe I was helpless. Why? Part of it was overwhelm; the money stuff felt too big, too complicated. Part of it was privilege, which is gross to admit, but true; there had always been a net, even if only an emotional one, and I'd used it at many points to put off growing up. Part of it was basic straight-up denial; I couldn't, or wouldn't, see what I'd created. But the biggest part—and what hit me hardest in that moment—was that I had been clinging to a fantasy. The fantasy that, eventually, someone was going to come along and save me. A man, specifically. I was waiting for a fucking man to save me. Underneath that fantasy, of course, was the belief that I couldn't handle this myself. And there were legitimate, understandable reasons for why I clung to that fantasy: the patriarchy, my father's blatant misogyny, Disney. But I didn't see any of that then, and it didn't matter anyway. The only thing that mattered was that I finally heard this. *No one is coming to save you, Laura.*

Maybe this story feels familiar. Even if our circumstances are different or money isn't something you've put your head in the sand about, perhaps there are other areas of your life that feel too overwhelming to look at. Maybe your drinking feels this way, or all the feelings *underneath* your drinking—all the stuff you know you'd have to face if you stopped—seem like far too much. In my experience, the anticipation of how terrible it will be to face these things is always far worse than the reality of facing them. Like the idea of putting all that debt on paper and arriving at the total number; it made me nauseous at first, but pretty quickly I began to feel relief. Because at least I knew. At least I wasn't hiding anymore. Like alcohol, our blame stories never protect us; they only give us the temporary illusion of protection.

These three stores—Jim's, Lisa's, and mine—are different versions of what I like to call Sneaky Blame Stories, or Sneaky BS. *Sneaky* because they're hard to spot. Our egos do a great job of hiding them. But they can't survive our honest scrutiny. Somewhere in there, we *know*, and what I'm asking you to do now is call your own Sneaky BS out. They are your roller skates and you've got to identify them so you can take them off.

> **QUESTIONS:**
>
> *When it comes to my alcohol use, what are my Sneaky Blame Stories?* If you're sober, apply this question to other parts of your life.
>
> *What have these blame stories kept me from confronting, accepting, or doing?*

WHAT'S BEHIND THAT?

Christopher Avery is the founder of the Responsibility Process. He has a PhD in behavioral science and more than twenty-five years of experience working in organizations to understand why so many employees are unhappy at work. In the course of his work, he came up with a beautiful question that points to how one can take responsibility in any scenario.

It is this: *How am I choosing, creating, or attracting this situation?*

At first, this question can feel super confrontational. *What do you mean I'm choosing to be in severe debt, without a car, unable to take my daughter to school? What do you mean I'm choosing to fight with my ex-husband to the point of tears? Or what do you mean I'm choosing to be addicted to alcohol?*

To be crystal clear, again, I'm not saying that people who are victims of, for example, abuse or sexual assault are responsible for what happened to them. That they somehow chose, created, or attracted those situations. Instead, I'm saying that we have some degree of choice as to how we respond to these traumatic experiences down the line. These events often have a ripple effect that go on to impact our lives forever, until we become conscious of the patterns they've created and we do the work to interrupt them. As we talked about previously, patterns of addiction and trauma are passed down through generations. I'm offering you a way to interrupt those patterns through conscious inquiry. It's not about taking blame or placing it elsewhere; it's about owning what we can control and letting go of what we cannot.

Let's explore some of the most common reasons we might choose, create, or attract situations and patterns that are painful and destructive. Keep in mind these are largely subconscious processes we've developed to keep us safe and alive, both physically and psychologically, or are the result of our environment and conditioning (and sometimes our genetics). In other words, these coping mechanisms arise from an adaptive, intelligent place within us—but they don't ultimately help us heal and evolve. Once we become aware of these things, we can answer the bigger question: *What's behind that?*

Familiarity—Simply put, humans seek what's familiar and predictable. Even when what's familiar and predictable is ruinous and painful. It's the whole *devil we know* thing. This is a pervasive psychological phenomenon known as "repetition compulsion," where a person repeats a traumatic event or its circumstances over and over again, including reenacting the event or putting oneself in situations where it's likely to repeat. According to Bessel van der Kolk, "Many traumatized people expose themselves, seemingly compulsively, to situations reminiscent of the original trauma. These behavioral reenactments are rarely consciously understood to be related to earlier life experiences." For example, my parents' divorce and the subse-

quent five divorces between them caused me to create drama
and instability in my own relationships. My friend Caroline's
father suffered from addiction, and she perpetually attracts addicted partners. Another friend's parents paid attention to him
only when he achieved something at school or in sports, so he
continually chases external rewards as validation in his relationships and at work. And my friend Tonia was abandoned by her
mom when she was young so she became overly clingy and anx-
iously attached in her relationships, which—until she did some
work on this in therapy—continuously drove people away, re-
creating her original abandonment.

QUESTIONS:

*Can I identify painful patterns in my relationships? Is
there a role I seem to continually fall into playing, or a
dynamic that shows up repeatedly?*

*When I consider these patterns, can I trace them back to
formative relationships or events in my childhood?*

*What are some of the beliefs I developed in those for-
mative relationships?* For example: *I don't deserve to
be treated well; people aren't to be trusted; everyone
leaves me.*

*Can I see connections between these beliefs and my
drinking? What are they?*

Limiting Beliefs / Fixed Mindset—In her seminal book
Mindset, Dr. Carol Dweck describes how the view we have of
ourselves profoundly influences the way we shape our lives.

Dweck explains that people who have a *growth mindset*—defined by the belief that intelligence, talent, and other qualities can be learned and developed over time versus those who have a *fixed mindset* and believe these qualities cannot be changed— are far more resilient, optimistic, creative, at peace, and satisfied. In simple terms, people who *believe* they can change and grow are far more likely to *actually* change. Again, most of us aren't even aware of the subconscious limiting beliefs playing in the background of our minds because they're so familiar. Beliefs like *It's too late; I suck at this; I'm too old; I can't make this any better; It's always been like this; I'm not the kind of person who x, y, z.*

QUESTIONS:

Do I generally believe my intelligence, talent, and skills are fixed and cannot change (fixed mindset), or that these things can be developed and changed (growth mindset)? Where did these beliefs come from?

How have these beliefs impacted my life? Consider relationships, work, pursuit of goals/dreams.

What are the most consistent limiting beliefs I have? These may be immediately obvious to you, or uncovering them may require some time and observation. Examples: I'm too old/dumb/unqualified; It's too late; I'm not smart enough; I am bad; It's my fault; I am powerless; I'm not worthy; Resting is lazy.

How have these limiting beliefs negatively impacted my life and my perception of responsibility? For example:

I believed I wasn't smart or skilled enough to manage my finances, so I ignored the problem, blamed circumstances and other people, and accumulated massive debt.

Choose one of your limiting beliefs and write a counter-belief that is positive and growth oriented.

For example:

Limiting belief: I'm terrible at money.

Counter-belief: I'm learning to better manage my money every day.

Make sure you choose a counter-belief that is realistic. It should feel like a stretch, but not an impossibility. In the example above, "I'm amazing at managing money!" might feel too unbelievable, whereas "I'm learning to better manage my money every day," is more realistic (even if it feels challenging).

When you've arrived at a counter-belief, make an effort to practice it by saying it out loud in conversation, writing it down and putting it in different places where you can see it (bathroom, nightstand, computer screen, your phone screen), telling a few people you're working on shifting this specific mindset, and asking them to let you know when you slip into your limiting-belief language.

Confusing Duty or Obligation with Responsibility—This is a big one. Oftentimes, because of what we're taught grow-

ing up and the cultural messages we receive about what con-
stitutes a responsible, or "good," person, we conflate duty and
obligation with responsibility. Generally speaking, women tend
to learn that responsibility means duty, service, and putting
the needs of others first no matter the cost to oneself. Men, on
the other hand, generally tend to associate responsibility with
providing and being "strong," or not showing vulnerability or
weakness. So we act out these roles as we're expected to, and
we get caught up in lots of "shoulds."

In my own case, when I became a mother, I believed I
should be able to keep all the other parts of my life going
at full capacity—my career, my home, my friendships, my
marriage, everything—as I had before. *And*, that I should feel
grateful for the opportunity to "have it all," oh, and also—
I should look great while doing it! I believed this because this
is what society tells women. This is what responsibility looked
like. But here's the miss: True responsibility never comes from
abiding by a should. When we do something because we feel
like we "should," we're always living according to someone
else's values, someone else's script. That's duty. That's obligation. But it's not responsibility. Responsibility comes from the
conscious decision to choose, and to know *why* we are choosing. It's a subtle but crucial difference.

Taking responsibility doesn't mean we always *like* what we
choose to do. We may find something awful and unpleasant,
but still choose to do it because it's important to us, aligns with
our values, or is truly not within our control. But doing that
same thing out of blind duty and obligation because we feel
like we should or we have to is a totally different vibe. Respon-

sibility creates freedom (if only in our mind); duty and obligation create resentment.

QUESTIONS:

*In which areas of my life do I feel a heavy sense of
"should"?* Note: These are areas where you may tend to
have a lot of resentment and anger, and/or guilt when
you consider *not* doing what you "should." For example: "I
should make healthy meals for my family every night," or
"I should just be grateful for this job," or "I should visit my
elderly parents every weekend." *Don't judge your statements as right or wrong; just be honest.*

*Where did the ideas of what I "should" do come from?
Does each "should" reflect my beliefs and values, or did
I inherit it from someone or something else?*

*For the "shoulds" that don't belong to me, what feelings
come up when I consider going against them?*

What is the price of continuing to abide by these "shoulds"?

*Do I see a connection between my "shoulds" and my
alcohol use?*

Fear of (Perceived) Pain—Nearly everything destructive
we do can be traced back to fear in some way. The list of things
we fear is endless, but they can all be boiled down to one thing:
fear of pain. We don't want to risk loving someone because we
fear the pain of losing them. We don't risk trying something
new because we fear the pain of failing. We don't start some-

thing because we fear the humiliation of not finishing. We drink because we fear the pain of feeling our shame, our anger, our sadness, or the vulnerability of our joy. We don't *stop* drinking because we fear the pain of not belonging, being boring, being unable to cope—and so on and so on forever. From the moment we are born until the moment we die, we're more or less dancing the same dance against pain—trying to decrease it, minimize it, get out of it—and rightfully so. Pain hurts. But there are two important things we need to understand:

1. Pain can ultimately never be avoided.
2. We are terrible judges of what will make us feel better *and* worse in the future. We tend to catastrophize how bad we will feel when we do something challenging (such as tell the truth to our partner) and how good we will feel when we get something we want (for example, have the drinks / get the raise / win the fight).

Knowing these things, we can begin to let go of the fantasy that pain can ever truly be avoided, and face the fears that are keeping us from making positive choices.

QUESTIONS:

The below questions are specific to alcohol use. If you're already sober, substitute another "thing" that's keeping you stuck and causing you pain.

What pain do I believe alcohol helps me cope with?

What pain does drinking cause me?

What am I afraid will happen if I stop drinking?

What am I afraid will happen if I continue drinking?

What do these questions reveal to me?

Incapacitation—When I first read about incapacitation in Steven Pressfield's book *Turning Pro,* I cringed with recognition. He writes that during World War I, it was not uncommon for soldiers to take their rifles and literally shoot themselves in the foot. They'd claim it was accidental, but they did it in hopes of avoiding the trenches. Pressfield says, "The habits and addictions of the amateur are conscious or unconscious self-inflicted wounds. Their payoff is incapacity." Incapacity. *Ouch.* It's true: When I was incapacitated by being drunk or hungover, I didn't have the space or energy to actively participate in my life. I was conveniently distracted by all the messes I'd made—the drama, the chaos of being on roller skates. I can see all my self-defeating behaviors in this way—from drinking to love addiction to overworking to overspending— were about this, in some sense. It was all one big elaborate subconscious effort to incapacitate myself so I didn't have to face the truth of what I wasn't doing, what I wasn't becoming.

QUESTIONS:

Can I see my drinking as a way to incapacitate myself? If you're already sober: Can I see other ways I incapacitate myself?

What is this incapacitation keeping me from dealing with?

What is this incapacitation keeping me from becoming?

While the above list certainly doesn't cover *every* reason we might choose, create, or attract painful situations and patterns and thus, as Christopher Avery says, stay "below the line of responsibility," it does illuminate a lot. Knowing there are real factors driving our behavior helps to make sense of our seemingly nonsensical actions. And we can then begin to feel compassion for ourselves and our shortcomings. One of the most helpful things I learned from Christopher Avery is that we are naturally wired *not* to take responsibility; it's a defense mechanism. But, conversely, we are also wired *to* take responsibility. We just have to learn what it actually means and looks like, versus what we are often taught (duty, obligation, being "good," and following the rules).

Of all the skills I've developed in sobriety, learning to take responsibility for my experience has been the most life changing. It's also the most annoying and, frankly, rude. The lessons of responsibility keep knocking and knocking and knocking on the door until they're heard, and as far as I know, it's like this for everyone. Like finding myself riding in the back of a police cruiser at two years sober because I was still burying my head in the sand about money, realizing that my people-pleasing tendencies played a part in every friendship I found challenging, and, in more recent years, discovering that sobriety wasn't going to magically resolve my painful relationship patterns with men.

But despite the annoying rudeness, I mean it about being life changing. Responsibility forces me to look at any situation with clear eyes and ask myself: *Is this something I want to continue feeling, doing, or being part of? What is my part in it? How am I making it better, or worse? What choices do I have, and am I willing to make them?* This last question is the money shot. We always have some kind of choice, even if it's only to hold something or someone differently in our mind—to begin telling ourselves a different story about it—one that is less harmful, painful, and destructive to our well-being. I'm not saying it's easy; sometimes, this kind of choice is among the hardest we will ever have to make.

But over the years, I've learned this: Whenever I talk about responsibility in sobriety, either in TLC meetings or at a book event, the response is typically twofold: First, people are annoyed, and then they're relieved. I think this is because we know that as long as we refuse it, we'll stay stuck, circling the same old cul-de-sac of victimhood on our roller skates, waiting for someone or something to guide us home. But we *also* know that when we decide to finally remove those things from our feet and take that first step on solid ground everything changes. The whole world opens up.

3

IT IS UNFAIR THAT
THIS IS YOUR THING.

"LAURA, IT'S TIME TO JUST GIVE *UP*."

My friend Mark and I were sitting at our local pizza place after our usual Saturday night twelve-step meeting.

"What?"

He smiled. "Just give up. Stop *trying* so hard. You don't have to prove anything. I see you struggling to say the right thing, and you don't have to. It's not gonna help."

I had shared at the end of the meeting because I was committed to doing things differently. After trying to get sober for over a year, I finally had a little bit of time under my belt— a couple of months. But I had never stayed sober for that long before, and one of the things I had been doing—following the advice of others—was speaking up in meetings. As much as I hated it and felt like throwing up every time, I was forcing myself to do it.

"That obvious, huh?" I laughed and felt my face flush.

"At some point, we all have to give up performing. I know you're strong, capable, smart—all that shit—we *all* know that! But you're also struggling and scared and you won't admit it. You don't think we see it? Of course we do. So just give up. Give up the show."

UGH. He was right, and I hated that he could tell—that they could all tell.

The server brought our pizza over, and we started to dig in.

After a few bites he laughed and said, "I mean . . . is it working?"

"No . . . fuck! No, it's not *working*, asshole."

"Exactly." He laughed. "So give up."

"But . . . *how?*"

"Try this. What would you say if you weren't trying to be strong? What would you say if you told the truth?"

"About what?"

"About how you feel right now."

I put down my slice.

"Right now . . . I'd say *I hate this*. I honestly hate it. I hate that this is what I'm doing every Saturday night. That it's what I have to do. No offense."

"Keep going."

"And . . . I'm angry all the time, but I feel like I have no right to be. I'm jealous and hateful of everyone who can have a regular fucking Saturday night. I'm tired of thinking about drinking or not drinking or what I'm feeling all the goddamn time. It's exhausting! It all feels so unfair."

He put down his slice, leaned back, and double fist-pumped the air. "There you go. Keep doing *that*."

At home later that night under my covers, I replayed our conversation in my mind and found myself crying, which surprised me. Even though I felt sad, frustrated, and angry a lot of the time, I rarely cried. Tears had never come easy for me, and although that was a point of pride, sometimes it secretly worried me. I could go months and months without crying. One of the gifts of drinking was it allowed me to access this part of myself. Every so often I'd find myself too many drinks deep, sobbing to a friend or on the phone with my mom late at night, usually about how bad I wanted to find "my person" (something I would never allow myself to say sober). They were sloppy, booze-fueled tears, but they were better than nothing.

I hadn't realized how hard I'd *still* been hustling to hold up this idea of being strong. Capable. Smart. Like I *had* this sobriety thing. Like I knew what to do. Like I didn't need help. I thought I had let go, but apparently I hadn't. Mark was right: I was trying to prove something all the time. To myself. To the people in those rooms. To everyone. It was a very, very old act and so ingrained I didn't even know I was doing it.

Of all the things I'd said to Mark, the part that tugged at me hardest, the part that kept reverberating in my body, causing my throat to swell into a tight knot when I replayed it, was the admission that this felt unfair. It reminded me of a line from Caroline Knapp's *Drinking: A Love Story*, the first recovery memoir I'd ever read. Of all the exquisite writing in that book, all the ways she so tenderly and perfectly described the slow, elusive becoming of addiction, all the heavy moments of despair and isolation and denial and grief, there was one small moment—a relatively banal one, considering—that had made me strangely emotional when I read the book for the first time a decade earlier. Caroline is recounting the early days of so-briety and a Saturday night when her friend Abby came over for dinner, barging into the house, clutching two bottles of seltzer water. "This sucks!" Abby said. "It's a fucking Saturday night and I just want to sit at the table and drink red wine. It *sucks* that I can't do that!"

The scene pierced me both then and now, I realized, be-cause it was the kind of raw display of vulnerability I would never allow, certainly not in front of other people. It would have (I thought) exposed me as childish, self-pitying, and stupid, even though when I read it in Caroline's story I only recognized it as honest. I remember being *afraid* of feeling that way when I had read it so long ago, as if it was a preview of the inevitable. What I hadn't understood at the time, though, was what exactly it was that I had been so afraid of. It wasn't only seeming childish or self-pitying or stupid or weak: Those were the surface things. It was what lived underneath that had me panicked—the unstop-pable weight pulling me down into the river: It was grief. The incredible sadness of all I was losing by losing drinking.

· ·

Until that point, I hadn't allowed myself to see what I was going through as grief. *Why?* Mostly because I thought I had no right to it.

Going back to my conversation with my friend Grant a year before, when he told me I wasn't bad, but *sick*, and that it wasn't my fault, any more than it would be my fault if I had cancer, the idea of feeling grief was contradictory to what I thought I was allowed to feel. Grief is a process we culturally acknowledge when someone loses something important, but we don't tend to allow people to feel grief when we think people *deserve* the loss. For example, if someone in a relationship commits infidelity and the relationship ends, we generally feel that the person who was cheated on is the only one allowed to grieve. Or, if someone loses a job, for example, we'd want to know why they lost it before we decide whether or not the person has any right to feel grief about the loss. We have rules about who is and isn't allowed to feel pain based on unspoken and internalized beliefs about fairness and justice. People who make choices that incur a loss generally don't have the right to feel grief, while people who suffer from circumstances out of their control do. And embedded into those rules are even more rules. While we acknowledge losing someone close to us as a cause for grief, if someone loses a parent who is older, say, in their nineties, we tend to see that as a lesser loss than losing a parent who is younger. Losing a child violates every law of natural order and deserves the maximum allotment of grief. And so on.

Culturally, we see addiction as something people do to themselves and the people around them. We see it as their fault. And so the message we internalize, what I internalized, was that I had no *right* to feel sad about it. How could I have compassion for myself or consider my feelings when I had behaved so selfishly and wreaked such havoc on the people around me—when I had "chosen" to drink again and again—despite all the wreckage? Besides, why would anyone mourn leaving something behind that is so clearly destructive to them and the people around them?

I'm not saying infidelity and job loss are the same thing as addiction. I'm simply pointing out that we abide by ingrained rules about who is allowed to feel grief and who isn't. About what is fair and what isn't. About what types of people have permission to mourn and what types don't. Outside of recovery circles (and even sometimes in them) people who fall into addiction aren't given permission to grieve. They're supposed to overcome, repent, fix, get their shit together—and to do it quietly, somewhere else, without inconveniencing everyone else. While I'm not denying the pain and trauma that ripple through the lives of the addicted, nor the responsibility to face and heal what we can, the idea that there's no real loss for us when we give up drinking, that we're not entitled to grieve because we've brought this upon ourselves, these are destructive, insidious lies. It's yet another face of the corrosive shame that keeps us bound and tortured in the cycle of addiction. Researcher and author Brené Brown says, "Shame needs three things to grow out of control in our lives: secrecy, silence, and judgment." Here, we see all three in spades, but particularly judgment. And so even if we're able to stop drinking, the shame continues to grow, and we continue to hold ourselves over the cross, believing we deserve it.

. .

There are so many reasons why addiction *is* unfair, and I'll touch on that, but not because I'm interested in making a case for unfairness. That's not really what any of us is asking for when we say something feels unfair. None of us *actually* believes life is fair, but we still act and operate as if it *should* be. What we're asking for when we say something is unfair, like I did with Mark earlier that night, is for someone to witness our sorrow. To acknowledge it as real. To say, *"Yes, this sucks, and I'm so sorry it's happening to you."* It's a deep, primal need to feel seen and heard and understood and cared for when we're in pain. It's why children cry out for their parents when they get hurt. It's why my daughter, even at thirteen years old, still asks me to sleep next to her when she doesn't feel well. It's why people gather for funerals when someone dies: not only to pay respect to the dead, but to witness and validate one another's shared pain.

When it comes to addiction, we perhaps need that validation even more—I certainly did—because we're so steeped in self-hatred and shame, believing not only that we've done this to ourselves, but that we've also done it to other people. Our internal monologue, born from what we're told by those around us, and what society tells us, is a never-ending ticker tape of: *you're so weak; you're so selfish; you're so fucked up; you've got no self-control; you're just a drunk; you're a mess; you're a liar; you don't deserve to be a mother; you don't deserve to be a father; what is your problem?; just stop; why can't you just STOP?*

We wouldn't think twice about offering empathy to the child who fell at the playground or the mourners at a funeral, or the person who gets injured in an accident, or loses their partner. But with addiction, we do. Here, we largely say *tough shit; your fault; fix it.*

I'm sure that's what you've heard, and how you talk to yourself, right?

After Caroline's friend Abby said "This *sucks!*," Caroline's response wasn't to convince her otherwise, or list out all the reasons she's better off sober. She just says, "I know. It *does* suck." When I said that this all felt unfair and Mark didn't correct me, like so many people had before—like I had been correcting myself internally all along—it was such a gift. That's because emotional validation is among the most powerful healing encounters we can have. As mindfulness teacher and therapist Tara Brach says, "The moment we believe [our pain] is wrong, our world shrinks and we lose ourselves in the effort to combat the pain." I don't know that I've come across a better description of addiction than that: *Losing ourselves in the effort to combat pain.* We all believe we were wrong to fall into addiction, but then there's the added "wrongness" of feeling any kind of pain about letting go of the addiction, giving up what we've clung to so tightly—and what has *worked*, by the way, and is completely socially acceptable and encouraged, and is still okay for other people, but now not us—and what has become so much a part of our identity, of how we have survived. Every way we turn, it's wrong. *We're* wrong. When someone validates how we feel, we get to feel, for once, as though we're not wrong. That perhaps we, too, are deserving of compassion and love. We get to feel human.

In the most basic terms, when we feel like someone cares about our suffering, it is healing. This is what I felt that night sitting across from Mark, eating pizza, and what had happened countless other times before with other sober people, each time chipping away at the castle wall of separateness and shame, until I could finally hear it. *Yes, I was allowed to feel loss about this. Yes, my pain is valid and real. Yes, someone cares about my suffering.*

Maybe you need to hear these things, too.

. .

For many of us, having our feelings invalidated or growing up in an emotionally invalidating environment is part of our original wounding. And we've adapted by rejecting, mistrusting, or feeling shame for our feelings when they don't seem "appropriate" and/or won't elicit the approval we crave and need.

In response, we do what all kids (and adults) do: We adapt.

My friend Eric learned achievement was the way to get his parents' attention and approval, so he became the best at everything he possibly could. He was the president of his high school class, the captain on every sports team he played on, graduated second in his class, and went on to apply himself in the same way professionally, becoming one of the youngest chief marketing officers in a global company by the age of thirty-four. "Nothing was ever enough," he says. "As soon as I achieved one thing, I was on to the next. It was always about the next level, the next accolade, and I required constant appreciation and acknowledgment, or else I felt empty."

Drinking was a huge part of Eric's social and work life. "I didn't think twice about it because everyone around me drank, a lot." Working in the pharmaceutical industry, like so many other "work hard / play hard" industries, meant free-flowing booze was an expected part of every trip, every client dinner, every night after a grueling day of work. "It was always there," he said. "Hangovers were a badge of honor, and as long as you got your shit done, nobody cared."

Eric, like so many people, thought the drinking was fun— and for a long time, it was. He wasn't doing anything different from anyone else around him. But over time, it started to affect his life. He was less present for his kids. He pushed boundaries at work, showing up hungover for important presentations. He spent more and more time out, under the guise of "work," away from his family. Faced with an ultimatum from his wife, he gave it up, and once it was gone, he realized how much he'd relied on it to cope with the enduring emptiness he'd always felt—the lack of self-worth and insecurities he'd been carrying around since childhood. "Drinking made it possible for me to stay 'above water' on those things, and when I stopped, I realized how scared, angry, and miserable I was, and how drinking had kept me from feeling those things for so long."

Another friend, Elissa, grew up an only child in seventies-era New York City. Her mom, a stage performer, was beautiful and enigmatic, as well as mentally ill, narcissistic, and hypercritical of Elissa, who was so different from her in every way—a studious, short, and sturdily built queer writer who couldn't be less concerned with glamour. Elissa's introduction to alcohol was through her beloved father. They would venture around their city, a team of two facing the world, bonding over conversation and drinks and the precarious nature of the third figure in their family. Elissa, like so many, came to equate alcohol with connection and love and ease and possibility, and as a guard against the pain of so much trauma—pain that would have otherwise crushed her. In this way, it became a friend, a confidant, the reliable port in a volatile world. Eventually, as happens, it started to hurt far more than it helped. In her fifties, her port had become a prison; what had once saved her would end up killing her if she couldn't find a way to let it go.

My friend Chris grew up as one of the only Black kids in his West Texas town. A shy, sensitive kid, he says the predominant feeling he had growing up was disconnection. Not belonging. He quickly realized alcohol helped; it eased his loneliness, dissolved his inhibitions, lifted his depression, and made him feel connected. But drinking got bad for him quick. By the age of twenty-five, Chris had two DUIs. He got sober, but everyone around him was carefree, partying, getting their legs under them as adults, and he felt more separate than ever before. "It was devastating," he says. "I thought I had found a way to cope with feeling so different, and then I had to give it up because it was clearly going to ruin my life."

I could tell hundreds of stories like this about people who start drinking and feel as though they're doing something right by partaking, by finding something that actually helps ease the disconnection and pain and loneliness and shyness and ugliness and awkwardness and insecurity and, in the process, makes life seem more fun and exciting and adventurous and smooth. They feel *normal*, and see evidence all around them that they are. And then, for reasons largely out of their control, they discover—*surprise, just kidding!*—they're actually doing it all wrong. Yes, you're supposed to do it, but not like *that*. You're supposed to pour this highly addictive substance down your throat but not get *addicted* to it. You're supposed to love it, but not *too* much.

Where's your self-control? Where's your dignity? Why'd you set off that invisible tripwire inside your brain? Why can't you just *stop*?

· ·

When people get sober, they don't only give up alcohol, they give up an entire identity. I started drinking when I was fifteen, during the most formative years of my life, and I didn't stop until I was thirty-six. That's over twenty years of learning how to move through life in a certain way, as a certain type of person. Without alcohol, I had to learn how to work, how to have a conversation, how to date, how to have sex, how to have fun, how to self-soothe, and how to sit with my feelings. I had to learn how to live, and not "all over again," because I'd never learned how to do many of these things: I had to learn them *for the first time.* I had to learn how to be bored. How to eat dinner in a restaurant, or at home, without drinking. How to come down from a day at work, or a hard conversation. I had to learn how to face my mistakes and regrets and shame without an anesthetic. I had to learn how to accept my body, my inadequacies, my humanity. I had to learn how to pay bills on time and open my mail and face the dumpster fire of my finances. I had to learn how to be a friend. I had to learn how to be a mother. I had to learn how to stop shielding myself with lies and begin to tell the truth. I had to learn what the truth even was. I had to learn boundaries. I had to learn to respect other people's boundaries. I had to accept that I could not be everything to everyone and that I could not "nice" my way into your liking me. I had to accept that some people simply will not like me. I had to accept that I simply did not like some people. I had to learn that criticism won't kill me. I had to learn how to breathe through anxiety, and loneliness, and overwhelm. I had to learn how to sit with joy—the most vulnerable emotion of all—and not be absolutely terrified of it, to not sabotage it, to not be consumed with waiting for it to disappear. I had to accept that I didn't have control over whether my heart would break.

This sucked, and it was hard, and it *hurt.*

. .

So, yeah. It is unfair that this is your thing.

Because life is unfair, yes. But also, because you don't *deserve* it. This isn't happening because you're a broken, bad, weak, selfish piece of crap (or whatever other self-punishing thing you think). This happened because *it happens.* It just . . . happens. You didn't ask for it and you aren't being punished. But it's yours.

If no one has told you yet, let me be the first: I see you.

This sucks, and I'm so sorry you're going through it. Your pain is valid, and your sorrow is real. I understand. I know. I mean, I *really, really* know.

Okay?

So, breathe. And then do it again. Let's keep going.

4

THIS IS YOUR THING.

THIS IS YOUR THING.

Do you feel that? I mean *really* feel it? Meaning, do you accept it—this thing with alcohol—do you accept that it's happening, that it has already happened? Do you know, in the deepest part of you, that there's not a single thing in your power you can do to reverse it and make it not so? Here's how you'll know: acceptance, at the core, feels like relief. It might hurt. It might feel like the heavy stone of grief dropped into your belly. It might make you constrict with fear. Oh, it probably feels *terrible*. But also: There is relief. You can feel it in your musculature, in the electrical charge of your cells, as all that energy you've been using to fight against reality returns. It is the exhale of resistance.

Go ahead. Close your eyes and say it.

This is my thing.

How does that land? *Does* it land? If you're not there yet, that's okay. It's what we've come here to do.

. .

Come and sit a little closer. Maybe grab a cup of coffee or a tea or whatever helps you feel more settled and willing to listen. I'm not going to tell you anything you don't already know, but I'm going to say a few things that might help you finally *hear* what you know.

Things are what I refer to as the big forces we face in our life: situations, challenges, patterns, internal or external events that bring us to the edges of ourselves and ask us to grow beyond them. But before we grow, these things whip us around, turn us inside out, and blow us apart. They kick our ass. Oftentimes, our things don't only break us; they require a death of sorts—we have to sacrifice something we thought we knew for sure: a story, an identity, a way of being, life as we know it.

Sometimes our things don't even belong to us: They belonged to our parents, or grandparents, or generations even further back, but we're carrying them now because nobody before us could or would move through them. As therapist and writer Stephanie Wagner says, "Pain travels through families until someone is ready to feel it." Things are always an invitation to a deeper way of living, but they never feel that way. They feel like problems. They feel like injustices. They feel like loss and anger and frustration. They feel personal and unfair. They feel like shit.

Like you, I've had more than one thing in my life. Body issues, food issues, people-pleasing, perfectionism, money, divorce, anxiety, depression, abuse, and, of course, alcohol. Alcohol was my thing for a long time. I'm not sure if it was a thing I was born with or a thing that developed over time or both (it was probably both), but what I do know is, when I started out drinking in my teens it wasn't much of a thing. Then it grew from being an occasional thing in my early twenties, to a bigger thing in my late twenties, to a *much* bigger thing after I became a mother in my early thirties, to a thing that nearly killed me by the time I was thirty-five.

At that point, drinking was the Most Urgent Thing. It had to be dealt with before I had a shot at dealing with anything else, and this is what I want you to hear: If drinking is your thing, whether you recognize it or not, whether you're "functioning" or not, even if you've never had any big consequences due to it, the trajectory of this thing only goes one way: *from bad to worse.* **It only ever gets worse.** In this way, it is the Most Urgent Thing for anyone whose life it's impacting. Sure, you might have a few more hours of escape and fun left to eke out. You may be able to delude yourself into thinking this thing is not that bad for another month, maybe even for years. But in the background, the compound interest is building. This thing is like a black hole; it pulls everything else in your life into it and swallows it up, until all the goodness and light have disappeared completely. So the question is not whether you need to accept this thing. The question is only, *Will you accept it now, or later?*

My ex-stepfather has had an issue with alcohol since I met him when I was in junior high, more than thirty years ago. It was obvious then, but not life-ruining. He was still functional: He worked, played golf, had close friends and decent relationships with his family, and was generally loving and fun to be around. Still, I know he knew his drinking was a thing. He knew not only because people told him it was—including my mom, his kids, and his close friends—but because he *knew*, internally, the way we always know. I could see it in his eyes.

He didn't stop, though. And as the years have passed, it's gotten much worse. The last time I saw him was at an event in 2020, and he was so drunk he could barely talk. It was both heartbreaking and infuriating. After that, I heard he tried to get sober, but ultimately went back to drinking, got another divorce, and had to move in with one of his kids. Most of his relationships, including the ones with his kids, are painful and strained, and his grandkids' primary memories of him are of him being drunk. Yes, it's still possible he could get sober, but it's a hell of a lot harder at seventy-five than forty, or fifty, or sixty. As much as we want to believe we get infinite tries, we don't.

My friend Dev, though, has a different story. Their drinking bothered them now and then, but it never would have appeared to be a problem to anyone in their circle, not friends or family or even their boyfriend. But it gnawed at them, consistently, over the years, and we talked about it a lot. They'd usually call or text after a night of one too many bourbons, lamenting having overdone it, feeling shame for something stupid they said or how they felt they acted. I was around them when they drank many, many times, at parties and dinners and concerts, and while I never saw them get obnoxious or visibly inebriated, I could tell it weighed on them. After I witnessed their mental gymnastics for a few years, one day at lunch, they asked me the same question they'd asked countless times before: "Do you think I have a problem with alcohol?"

1. Have you ever decided to stop drinking for a week or so, but lasted only for a couple of days?

2. Do you wish people would mind their own business about your drinking—stop telling you what to do?

3. Have you ever switched from one kind of drink to another in the hope that this would keep you from getting drunk?

4. Have you had to have an eye-opener upon awakening during the past year?

5. Do you envy people who can drink without getting into trouble?

6. Have you had problems connected with drinking during the past year?

7. Has your drinking caused trouble at home?

8. Do you ever try to get "extra" drinks at a party because you do not get enough?

9. Do you tell yourself you can stop drinking any time you want to, even though you keep getting drunk when you don't mean to?

10. Have you missed days of work or school because of drinking?

11. Do you have "blackouts"?

12. Have you ever felt that your life would be better if you did not drink?

These questions are useful to a degree, but in my opinion they are too narrow in scope, and don't address the more hidden, inner experience of what it is to have this thing.

Here are some additional questions I suggest sitting with. This isn't a scientifically tested quiz. There's no official num-

ber of yes answers that will tell you if this is your thing. It may
be that only one yes is enough, or it may be twenty. Again, the
only person who gets to say what's true for you is you. These
questions are based on my own experience and the experience
of sitting with, talking to, and connecting to thousands of others who've struggled with this thing.

1. Have you made promises to yourself about drinking
less or not drinking at all?

2. Have you found it difficult or impossible to keep those
promises?

3. Does alcohol factor heavily into the plans you make?
For example, do you avoid making plans in places where
you won't be able to drink? Or do you specifically plan
things where alcohol won't be involved to keep yourself
from drinking?

4. Do you prefer spending time with people who drink
or won't judge your drinking?

5. Do you monitor how much you and others are drinking when you're in a social situation?

6. Have you justified the consequences of your drinking
more than once?

7. Is alcohol one of the first things you reach for when
you're uncomfortable, bored, lonely, angry, hungry, excited, happy, overwhelmed, sad, or tired?

8. Do celebrations feel incomplete without alcohol?

9. Have you looked for proof that your drinking isn't
that bad—for example, found other people with bigger
or worse consequences?

10. Have you done a Google search about problematic

drinking, how you know you're an alcoholic, or what sobriety is like?

11. Do you have a hard time focusing in conversations or social situations unless you have a drink in your hand or know when the next one is coming?

12. Have you worried about how much you like to drink?

13. Do you plan around your hangovers—for example, not scheduling work meetings early in the morning?

14. Do you truly enjoy doing things where alcohol isn't involved?

15. Are you anxious, irritable, and agitated if you can't drink when you want to?

16. Do you rush through making dinner, bedtime routines with your kids (if you have them), or other activities so you can get to the part where you can drink?

17. Does almost everyone you know drink?

18. Do you feel like you'd lose your social life if you stopped drinking?

19. Is drinking a major part of your significant relationships?

20. Do you feel like life would be far less exciting, fun, or tolerable without alcohol?

21. Do you rely on alcohol to "come down" from your day (even if it's not every day or most days of the week)?

22. Do you rely on alcohol to get to sleep?

23. Do you feel like certain experiences, such as birthdays, anniversaries, holidays, vacations, promotions, or weekends, aren't "complete" unless you drink?

24. Do you have difficulty being intimate or having sex without some alcohol in your system?

25. When was the last time you've gone thirty days or more without consuming alcohol?

26. When you consider going more than thirty days without drinking, do you feel anxious, uneasy, or scared?

27. Do you feel a palpable sense of relief when you know it's almost time to drink?

28. Have you hidden how much you drink from people around you?

29. Have you ever snuck drinks when nobody was looking?

30. Do you make extra efforts to hide your drinking or act like it's not a big deal for you?

31. Do you post, share, or like memes about drinking to normalize it?

32. When other people laugh about their escapades, make jokes about drinking a lot, or encourage overdrinking, do you feel relieved?

Okay, now, if you're still wavering and unsure after all that, then ditch all those questions and focus on one. Because behind all the calculating and thinking and justifying and denying and weighing and comparing—whether you've never suffered a single consequence, or you've lost every single thing that matters to you—this is the one question none of us can escape:

Are you free?

Read it again.

Are you free?

I'm not talking about freedom to do whatever you want, whenever you want. I'm not talking about being able-bodied or a certain size or never feeling the strong pull to eat more, sleep more, drink more, laugh more, cry more, work more, or fuck more than you know is good for you. I'm not talking about having the dream job, a job you even mildly like, or any job at all. I'm not talking about never feeling sad, or angry, or jealous.

What I'm talking about is not the kind of freedom anyone else can grant us or take away: not our partners, our parents, our children, our friends, our bosses, our communities, or our governments. What I'm talking about is an internal, intractable freedom. The kind Dev got, the kind I have, the kind anyone who faces their thing gets. It's the freedom of not being owned by an addiction, and thus, having access to what's best in you. It's being able to actively *respond* to life instead of just reacting out of fear, shame, or regret. It's being able to trust yourself to follow through when you make promises and plans. It's knowing your word actually means something, and moving through your days with some dignity. It's showing up instead of hiding and telling the truth instead of lying. It's having command over how you spend your energy, your heart, *your life*.

Ask yourself, does alcohol own your attention even a *little* bit more than you want it to? Does the pull to escape, to heighten, to numb, or to otherwise alter the direct experience of life win out more often than not? When it comes to drinking, are you genuinely able to choose? In this way, are you free?

When I was drinking, I could have wiggled my way out of answering yes to most of the above questions, could have used them to convince myself I wasn't bad enough to have to stop, even right up to the very end when I was shaking and sick all the time. But this question? *Am I free?* This one hits differently. This one is hard to hide from. I was never free when it came to alcohol; it owned some sacred part of me from the start. I knew by the way I loved it: a little too much. A possessive, obsessive love. A love that felt like need. Drinking took away more and more of my freedom, and above all else, this is what made it my thing.

· · ·

Okay, so even if we *know* this—if we can see *so clearly* that this is our thing—then why would we work so hard to deny it? Why would we do everything in our damn power to avoid facing this one thing? There are many reasons, but I think they can be boiled down to four key points. I'm laying these out so you can hear yourself in them, and in hearing them, perhaps you will start to realize how common, futile, and false these defenses are.

FOUR REASONS WE DENY THIS IS OUR THING

1. We will do just about anything to avoid feeling pain.
2. We're terrified of not belonging.
3. We're afraid life will suck without alcohol.
4. We're ashamed of what this thing means about us.

WE WILL DO JUST ABOUT ANYTHING TO AVOID FEELING PAIN.

The lengths to which we, meaning humans, will go to avoid pain can't be overstated. Unconsciously and consciously, our baseline behaviors are pain avoidant. It's a time-honored truth, not unique to you or me or anyone else. It's the reason the Buddha's first lesson, or the First Noble Truth of Buddhism, is that pain and suffering (dukkha) are endemic to the human experience. We will all experience various levels of pain and suffering so long as we are alive, and resisting it, believing it shouldn't be so, or attempting to stop it is pointless and only causes more suffering. It is ironically only through acceptance of our pain that it begins to shift.

The problem with using alcohol to numb our pain is that while it may work temporarily, it always, *always* adds more pain in the end. Whatever we may gain in temporary relief is multiplied with suffering in return. As the saying goes, "It's hard to get enough of something that almost works." So in an attempt to avoid pain we only create more, not realizing that *the elimination of pain is a futile enterprise,* whether we are drinking or not. Yes, it's painful to get sober and feel our feelings and face our past and do the hard work of cleaning up our insides. But in sobriety, at least there's a payoff. In sobriety, at least we can put the inevitable pain of living to use. We can let the pain move through us, and allow it to change us in the ways we need to be changed and teach us what we need to know. In this way, pain can be transmuted into wisdom.

WE ARE TERRIFIED OF NOT BELONGING.

My friend Mikel grew up in a violent home with an alcoholic father and a mother who was helpless to stop him. Ensnared by his addiction, his father shot himself in the head when Mikel was nineteen, and by the age of twenty-two, Mikel was ready to do the same. He got sober instead, and when he talks about his past and recounts his childhood, he says he suffered all kinds of violence, but the kind he felt most pervasively was what he calls "the violence of belonging."

Yes. The violence of belonging.

Mikel explains that the violence happened in two ways. There's the violence of what happens *to* you, and the violence of what happens *inside* of you as a result. At home, Mikel was physically and emotionally abused by his father. His dad punched, kicked, and hit him as a way of toughening him up and making him "a man."

"There was this constant refrain of 'You'll lose belonging to this family' if you don't act a certain way," Mikel says. "It wasn't always said explicitly, but it was implied at every turn. My hopes and dreams—essentially, who I was as a person—were ridiculed, crushed, and denied over and over. And of course I wanted to belong to my family. Of course I wanted their approval. I needed it." This was the first kind of violence: being forced to conform and the threat of being exiled from his family if he didn't comply.

Then there was the violence that happened inside of him: self-loathing, shame, and continual rejection of his needs and desires, which in turn caused him to inflict violence on himself through self-harming behaviors, including sabotaging relationships, allowing people to act out emotional violence on him in order to belong, and using drugs and alcohol.

Ironically—like so many people, myself included—alcohol becomes the gateway *to* belonging, however artificial. When we didn't or couldn't feel a part of a group, our family, or a community, alcohol provided the way in—functioning as both an anesthetic for the pain of disconnection and as a way to feel more connected. Seen this way, it's easy to understand why we can so quickly become dependent on it.

Mikel's story isn't unique. Although the details vary, almost everyone I know who's gotten sober echoes what he expressed about the violence of belonging. It's not true only for people who struggle with addiction, but it seems to be more acute for us. It's kind of the ultimate "gotcha!" Alcohol allows many of us to feel our first and only sense of belonging, and then when we're faced with getting sober, we're told the remedy is to extract ourselves from that belonging. So we feel we're being exiled once again, and it's not only a feeling or something we imagine; the otherness we face is real. We're "othered" into a small minority of the population who doesn't drink in an alcohol-obsessed world, and further "othered" by a label we're told we have to take on: the *addict*, the *alcoholic*, the person with a problem. But this time, we've got to face it sober. No medication. No numbing.

I mean. Who *wouldn't* avoid that?

But here's the truth (and this tracks with every single person I've met in recovery): It was *only in sobriety* that I came to truly belong. To others, yes, but more important, to myself. It didn't happen right away. It took time, and it took a willingness to stand in the fire, day after day, until eventually everything I'd known and relied on before had burned away. It took faith that I'd withstand the wretched burning. But it did happen; it always happens, eventually, if we stay. While it was initially terrifying to give up the false sense of belonging that alcohol gave me, it was the only way through to the actual thing. What I found on the other side of all those flames were the bigger, deeper, sturdier truths of life—ones that could actually sustain me. I found a ground I could stand on, a friend inside myself, a place I'd always belong.

As for the labels, you don't have to take them on. You just don't! The word "alcoholic" has never felt right in my mouth, even when I used it in the early days of being in AA to abide by the culture of meetings. So I don't use it. My experience was that there is often an overidentification with the label, a sort of overprescribing of what I see as totally human behavior (sensitivity, prone to resentments, a proclivity to extremes) as characteristic of an "alcoholic," and that didn't jibe with me. I say I'm sober, or that I don't drink. Lots of people I know like the label; they find it helpful and dig its subversiveness. Whatever works for you, do that. The point is you decide. You don't have to call yourself anything you don't want to call yourself because someone or a group of people says you have to. We don't expect people who get addicted to smoking cigarettes, or work, or any of the other thousands of things humans get addicted to, to forever call themselves addicts or x, y, z-aholics after they stop. Similarly, folks who recover from cancer don't call themselves canceraholics; they call themselves *survivors*.

WE'RE AFRAID LIFE WILL SUCK WITHOUT ALCOHOL.

For me and most people, life without alcohol seemed like a worst-case scenario. I thought no one would love me, that I'd be boring, that *life* would be boring: dull, gray, and flat.

But one of the most fascinating things about humans is

our inability to accurately predict what will make us happy. In fact, we're terrible at it. This is evidenced by the fact that most of us have absolutely *horrific* experiences with alcohol— so many that it's laughable we'd even tolerate being in the same room with the stuff, let alone pour massive amounts of it into our mouths. And yet like that ex we can't stop going another round with despite the utter pile of misery we inevitably become with them, we get far enough from the pain and, as Taylor Swift sings, "I forget about you long enough to forget why I needed to."

There are many layers to the "why" behind this (attachment disorders, how substances hijack our pleasure-reward system, trauma, and so on), but at the most basic level, a simple, observable fact of human psychology is this: We forget how things *really* make us feel. As researcher and author of *Stumbling on Happiness* Daniel Gilbert says, "Our inability to recall how we really felt is why our wealth of experiences turns out to be a poverty of riches."

Another factor here is a phenomenon called "the End of History Illusion." In 2013, Gilbert, along with researchers Jordi Quoidbach and Timothy Wilson, conducted an extensive study of more than nineteen thousand people between the ages of eighteen and sixty-eight. They asked a series of questions designed to get at whether the subjects thought they had changed much in the past, and whether they believed they would change in the future. The results across the board, regardless of age, were the same: People uniformly believed they'd grown and changed in the past, but when it came to the future, they predicted they wouldn't change at all. In other words, we believe history ends here in this moment—that all we'll experience in the future is what we're experiencing right now. Especially when we're in pain.

I know I felt this in early sobriety, but also at the onset of every heartbreak, about every day in my first two years of motherhood, and I still feel it when I get the flu. Going through a hard time is rough as it is, but it's the unconscious panic that you will *always feel this way* that makes us suffer. Simply learning this is a thing our brains do is helpful because we can then catch it and call it out. When I notice it, I call it catastrophizing. It doesn't take away the pain, but it lifts a bit of the suffering.

Just as we're wrong about alcohol being our key to belonging, we're wrong to think life will suck without alcohol. As I wrote in *We Are the Luckiest,* "Now I feel about sobriety much the same as I feel about becoming a mother: It has brought me right up to the nose of life and forced me to look it straight in the face. At first, the nearness was too much; there was nothing to protect me from the immediacy of things—not the bright lights or the sharp pain. But then, eventually I came to see that this is what it really means to be alive—to not look away from any of it—and that all I was doing before was pretending: floating through my days half-numb, half-involved, half-awake, thinking I was really living when in fact I was missing it all."

Life doesn't suck without alcohol. Life is life whether we're drinking or not. It's just that when we drink, we miss all it can be.

I'm going to guess some of you might read that and think, *Okay, that **sounds** great and all, but what do I actually do with these* *very real fears in the meantime? How do I cope with losing the sense of belonging and connection that alcohol provides?*

One practice I learned in therapy is a form of written visualization where you play two different tapes forward. Imagine any scenario that feels to you like it would be incomplete, awkward, boring, or sad if you weren't drinking: dinner at home, eating out with friends, happy hour, a date, a concert, watching football. Now, in as much vivid, sensory detail as possible, write out each of the scenarios, one at a time: one where you go through the event drinking as you usually would, and one where you don't drink. It's important to write these down because it forces you to slow down.

I'll use myself as an example and sketch out what dinner with friends would look like drinking versus sober.

Drinking Scenario: I have two or three drinks at home before driving to the restaurant. When I show up, I'm already buzzed. I am excited to see my friends, but mostly focused on where my next drink is coming from, and I'm agitated that the server isn't coming fast enough. I spaced grabbing a card for my friend's birthday—which is the reason we're all having dinner—but I figure she won't care, she's busy, too, she gets it. When we sit down, I make an extra effort to act nonchalant about what we're going to drink, but it's all I can think about. When we order, I get a vodka soda because it's stronger than wine, even though I hate the taste. I drink it too fast and no one else is even close to finishing their drinks, but I'm ready for another. When the waiter comes over, I discreetly point to my glass to signal a refill, hoping no one else notices. By the time our entrées come, I'm drunk. Fast-forward several hours and I wake up in my clothes on my couch at three A.M. with a raging headache and my heart pounding. I look around in panic trying to piece together what happened. The last thing I vaguely remember is eating some kind of chocolate dessert. *How'd I get home? Where's my purse?* I scramble to find my phone and brace myself as I enter the passcode. I see texts from one of my friends who was at dinner, **You ok? Did you get home?** An hour later, **Laura??? I have your car keys.** I have a flash memory of riding in an Uber. *Fuck.* I don't have the stomach to read the rest of the texts yet. I get up and pound a huge glass of water with four Advil, take my clothes from last night off, and try to go back to sleep in my bed. After three hours I realize I'm not going to be able to go back to sleep, and I give up. I pay $75 for an Uber to take me to my friend's house to get my car keys, and then have the Uber take me to the restaurant parking lot. I text my other friends to apologize. It's a beautiful, sunny day but I spend it inside until it's time to go pick up Alma from her dad's—she'll be with me for the week. I had meant to go to the grocery store before I grabbed her but felt too rotten to go, so we order takeout again.

Sober Scenario: I show up at the restaurant on time and bring a card and a small gift for my friend's birthday—a new plant for her apartment. When we sit down at the table and look at the menu, I feel a little pang of sadness about not ordering wine, but once I have my club soda and lime in hand, it passes. I look through the food menu, getting excited about what I'm going to order, taking my time to pick out things I actually like. My stomach rumbles so loud we all hear it and laugh. I feel a little quiet and awkward for a while—the words don't flow as easily and it's like my conversation timing is off—

but I take some deep breaths and focus on listening. We order dinner and everything tastes incredible: the bread, the appetizers, my entrée. My friends sip their drinks but slow down after two rounds. One of my friends isn't even drinking at all; she ordered a Diet Coke. We talk about all kinds of things: kids, work, home. I notice one of my friends seems more quiet than usual, and I make a mental note to text her later and see if she's okay. We decide on dessert and I get my favorite: flourless chocolate cake. It's dense and bitter and perfect. When we pay the check, two of my friends decide they want to go to the place across the street for another drink, but I pass. I'm tired and can't wait to get into bed. We hug before we part ways and I'm overwhelmed by how much I love these people. When I get home, I brush my teeth, wash my face, put on my new pajamas, get into my bed, and revel in the glorious smell of clean sheets. I recall the conversations over dinner and send that friend a text, asking her if she's all right, that she seemed a little quiet. She thanks me for noticing and we make plans to chat in the morning over coffee. I drift off to sleep with a clear heart and a peaceful mind.

I wake up early without an alarm, and as I'm sipping my coffee, I text my friend. She catches me up on what's going on and we make plans to go for a walk later in the week. Before I pick up Alma at her dad's, I stop by the grocery store to pick up what we need for the week. We order takeout, but I don't feel guilty about it. Pizza sounds perfect.

If you're not sober yet, you'll have to stretch a bit to imagine the sober scene, but that's the point. Imagine all that's possible, what you'd *like* to feel, how connected and alive and present you *could* feel.

Your scenes may look totally different from mine, but I'm guessing the themes are the same. The fantasy you have about drinking and what it means for connection, fun, and ease is not at all the reality. The reality is messy, dark, disconnected, and ends in feeling sick, physically and emotionally. And, likewise, the ideas you have about what it'll be like to not drink are distorted. Yes, social situations might be awkward. Yes, you may feel like you don't know what to do with your hands. Some things simply aren't going to be fun sober, ever. Like, for me, sitting at a bar for hours doing nothing but keeping each other company while everyone slowly goes unconscious will never be fun again (if it ever was). And early on, you may have to bow out of certain things that might be awesome down the line when you're more comfortable, but not yet. Like concerts, or traveling—two things that were, for me, brutal in the beginning, but are infinitely more fun now than they ever were when I was drinking.

Once you've done this exercise a few times in writing, you'll find that these visualizations are easier to access internally when you need them—whether it's before going to a work dinner, going on a date, attending Thanksgiving at your aunt's house, or hosting your kid's birthday party.

Another simple practice that can be incredibly powerful is to make a list of people you admire, and what you admire most about them. I'm talking people you aspire to be like—true role models, icons, people you consider absolutely legendary. What do you admire about them? I've always admired writers—Joan Didion, Maya Angelou, Mary Oliver—but your list can include people in your everyday life, like your grandmother or your third-grade teacher. Consider whether their alcohol use had anything to do with why you admire them. Is it on their list of best character traits and accomplishments? And if you learned they didn't drink alcohol, would you admire them less, or more? When I'd be in a social situation and feel awkward, or feel sorry for myself for not going to the party, or like a big bore because my head was hitting the pillow at nine P.M. on a Friday—whatever it was that brought up that spiky feeling of loneliness or isolation and made me think, *Dammit, I just want to be like "everyone else"*—I'd think of my heroes and be reminded that *No. I absolutely do not want to be like "everyone else" in this way. I want to be exceptional, in the ways I see them as exceptional.* Doing this grounded me in the truth of what, and to whom, I really wanted to belong.

WE'RE ASHAMED OF WHAT THIS THING MEANS ABOUT US.

The last big reason we avoid accepting this as our thing is because we're ashamed. Back to the damn shame, right?

When my first book came out in early 2020, before the COVID pandemic hit, I traveled all over the United States talking to people about it. At the end of my talk, we'd do a Q&A. Over time, I noticed a recurring theme in the questions I received, questions such as: "How can I get my mother-in-law to stop judging me?" "Why isn't my partner more supportive?" "How do I not get hurt by people at work making fucking jokes about alcohol all the time?" "How do I get my friends to stop making me feel like shit about this?" My response was always to ask whether people in their life knew they were sober. And if that person was a partner, or someone close to them, I then asked if they'd *really* shared what it was like for them: how painful, how scary, how dark. Typically, the answer was *no*. I'd ask them why—why did they keep that part of their life hidden?

First, they'd say something about privacy or safety or otherwise look at me confused, never having considered the possibility of fully revealing themselves. Eventually, we'd land at the truth: They're ashamed. Ashamed that they have, as they see it, an ugly problem; that they weren't strong enough to stop it, that, as a woman I recently talked to—a successful writer and journalist, a mother and a wife—said about why she had never turned on her camera, displayed her real name, or raised her hand to speak in an online recovery meeting (this was in the days of COVID, when online meetings became the norm), "I can't bear to hear myself say that I'm a drunk." The judgments they're imagining other people have are actually their own. It's not about what their mother-in-law or their partner or their friends or their coworkers think about them; it's their own condemnation and judgment.

Then the next question: *How do I let it go? How do I let go of the shame?*

To this, I'd respond by asking whether they were ashamed of me. I'd say, *You've read my whole story. Are you embarrassed for me? Do you think I'm shameful?* This would always set off a surprised and emphatic, *No! No*, they'd say. *I think you're brave. I think you're amazing. I think you're a hero.* "Then how," I'd ask, "are you any different?"

We tend to think other people are different than we are. If

I laid out our experiences side by side and proved they were the same, you would still think, *No, I am the actual worst.* While you can see the humanity and redemption in my story, you still see yours as proof of what a piece of shit you are. And yet, they are the exact same stories. Even if the details are different.

If you have trouble letting this sink into your heart, imagine a person you love in an uncomplicated, pure way. Someone you effortlessly wish the best for. For them, your goodwill spills forth naturally, easily, and fully. For me, it's my daughter, but I can also feel this kind of love for my cats—for all the pets I've had in the past. Maybe yours is an animal, too. Bring that person or being into your mind and connect to the way you love them. Allow yourself to feel it fully.

Now imagine that this person or being feels the way you do about yourself. Imagine they hold this thing you're holding in the same heavy way you are: with biting judgment, self-hate, and shame. Imagine them thinking the thoughts you've thought about yourself or feeling the pain you feel. How would you hold them if they came to you? What would you say? What would come forth naturally?

Okay, now, I know you think what you're imagining and feeling is about *them*, but it's not, or at least it's not only about them. If what you experienced so easily—warmth, tenderness, empathy—came through for them, then it's in there for you, too. It's available for you to give to yourself. *This is the diamond in the center of your chest.* This is your Buddha-nature. The truest part of who you are. Bigger than any *thing* you might experience, including this one.

5

THIS WILL NEVER STOP BEING YOUR THING UNTIL YOU FACE IT.

IT'S ONE THING TO FINALLY SAY, *OKAY, THIS IS MY THING.* BUT IT'S not until we submit ourselves fully to the process of change— of *being* changed and all that it entails—that we actually begin to recover. If acceptance is the act of RSVPing "yes" to the party, *facing it* is when you decide to get dressed and, despite your terrible awkwardness and sweaty armpits, your fragile ego and your fear you'll be laughed out the door, you knock anyway. It's shaking hands with the intimidating host, stepping over the threshold, and throwing yourself into the middle of what Zorba the Greek called "the full catastrophe."

So the question, of course, becomes, *How?*

What does it mean to "face it"?

That's where we're going now. You've probably heard the phrase "Do the work." As in, if you want to heal, you've got to *do the work.* If you want results, you've got to *do the work.* Stuck, frustrated, not able to get sober or stay that way? *Do the work.*

While this whole book is meant to be usable and action-able, this chapter in particular is where I'll show you what *the work* actually looks like.

I've defined five core practices that I believe are the key to spiritual growth in sobriety. They are *acceptance, honesty, con-nection, embodiment,* and *service.* By "spiritual," I'm not referring to anything explicitly religious or theological, but rather the deepest level of our understanding—beyond, but not exclu-sionary of, the intellectual, mental, emotional, or physical. As I described earlier, the word *spirit* comes from the Latin word *spiritus,* which means breath, to breathe. When we understand something spiritually, it becomes part of us in the truest sense; we don't only know it, we *breathe* it. Similarly, the promise of recovery is not only to learn about things like acceptance, honesty, and service but to become them. Or, more accurately, to become a living *practice* of them.

I've called them "practices" because that's how I want you to look at these things: as something you commit to *slowly getting better at.* Practice—as opposed to, say, performance—implies a commitment to learning, not working toward some (impossible) final point.

. .

Often when people are new to sobriety or trying to put to-gether sober time and struggling, they think that "the work" they need to do is somewhere out there, beyond them. Recently, I was leading a sobriety support meeting and a woman named Nia, who'd just celebrated her second year of sobriety, was recounting how frustrated she'd been at her annual family vacation because she'd had a hard time being around so much drinking. She expressed disappointment in herself for feeling this way, and said, "Clearly, I have to do some work. If anyone has suggestions or resources for me, I'd really appreciate it."

In the same meeting, a man named Aaron shared that he was on day thirty, but that this was "maybe the hundredth time I've been here, so whatever." What Aaron didn't say, but what I knew, was that two years prior he was hospitalized for pancreatitis because of his drinking and was told if he didn't stop, he would die. That stay in the hospital was his first sober stretch in probably twenty years. He'd started drinking and doing drugs at fourteen, and by sixteen he was a daily user. Since his stay in the hospital, Aaron had had *far* more sober days than unsober ones. Yes, he'd slipped a few times, but, on the whole, his progression was miraculous. He consistently showed up in a sober community, made an effort to share in meetings and reach out to others, was in the process of completing his bachelor's degree, and had recently been promoted at work.

Both Nia and Aaron had made tremendous progress, and yet they still believed the starting point of "real sobriety" or "the work" was out there in the distance somewhere beyond them. What I said to them was this: *You are already doing it.* Nia didn't need "more resources" or "suggestions"—she'd been sober for two years and had just successfully survived a boozy family vacation! Sure, there were probably some things she could reflect on and process from the trip that might be helpful, but her uncomfortable feelings weren't a problem or an indication that she wasn't "getting it."

Similarly, Aaron's thirty days of sobriety wasn't a sign of failure. Two years ago he'd struggled to stay sober for thirty minutes, let alone thirty days. As long as he learned something from the experience and carried it forward, it was a win. Every hour, day, week, month he stayed sober he was learning and growing.

I want you to hear this message, too:

Not drinking through a boozy family vacation *is doing the work*.

Sitting with uncomfortable feelings instead of numbing out *is doing the work*.

Raising your hand in a support meeting and telling the truth about what's going on *is doing the work*.

Checking in with your sober friends *is doing the work*.

Reading this book right now *is doing the work*.

I'm willing to bet you're already *doing the work* in many ways, big or small.

Still, we all benefit from some structure and concrete practices, and that's what I will lay out here.

Before we begin, I want to remind you that this is work *all* humans have to do, not only people who experience addiction. Acceptance, honesty, and responsibility are qualities everyone should cultivate in order to build healthy relationships and find a sense of peace and meaning in their lives. But people in recovery *must* do this work. We can't afford to be unwell—the stakes are too high. As therapist and sober author

Veronica Valli says, "All humans are called to this work, it's just most people don't answer the call. But when you have a substance abuse problem, it forces you."

PRACTICE 1: ACCEPTANCE

After about a year of trying and failing to stay sober, I came across this passage in Augusten Burroughs's book *This Is How:*

> In 100 percent of the documented cases of alcoholism worldwide, the people who recovered all shared one thing in common, no matter how they did it: They didn't do it.

By "it" he meant drink. The only common denominator between the people who recovered from alcohol addiction was *not drinking alcohol.*

I had one of those soft-click moments when I read these words. I finally *got it.* I knew intellectually that sobriety meant abstinence. Not drinking. But somewhere deep inside, I was still searching for that damn third door.

For whatever reason, on that blazing hot July day in 2014, I was finally able to accept what I knew. Although I did drink a few more times after that, there was no relief left in it. The fantasy had died completely. If I was going to be sober, I had to stop drinking, period. Two months later, I was done for good.

This is how acceptance works. It's painful, but always, *always* less painful in the end. As author and spiritual teacher Caroline Myss says, "Having to say, 'If this is what I must accept, so be it,' can feel like chewing glass, but not being able to accept what you cannot change is like having to swallow those shards of glass." Accepting sobriety felt like chewing glass, but continuing to search for that third door would have been like swallowing the glass, and it would have no doubt yielded the same fatal result.

• •

Physical sobriety or sustained abstinence is the first (and if not the first, then certainly a necessary) part of what we must accept on the path to recovery. But then there's everything else. How do we learn to accept the infinite number of things we cannot control about life, like the passing of time, the fact of aging, getting sick (and people we love getting sick), our kids growing up, annoying coworkers, controlling bosses, overbearing in-laws, natural disasters and bad weather, our parents' political beliefs, pandemics, and the rest of it? And, on top of that, how do we learn to accept ourselves, especially when other people don't? How do we learn to accept life *as it is*, when we're not numbing out with alcohol or something else? This is the central question of this practice.

Living life as it is means that we stop trying to bend reality to meet our individual wants and desires, and instead allow what's *already true to be true*, and thereby accept the flow of reality so we can operate *within* it, instead of *against* it. This refers to our individual situations, but also to the meta, natural laws of the universe that apply to everyone. Things like: People will disappoint and betray us; life doesn't always meet our expectations; we will win some and lose some; giving ourselves freely to love means we become vulnerable to the pain of loss;

people we love will die; our children are their own people; people get sick; not everything in life is fair or makes sense; the sun will rise and set every day, marking the passing of time over which we have no control; our bodies require food, water, and sleep; it will storm on days we don't want it to; choices have consequences; hard work pays off much of the time, but sometimes it doesn't; we cannot control anything about what other people do, think, or feel. And so on. While these things may sound elementary and obvious, most of us spend our lives denying and fighting against them. And if addictions can be seen as a way to cope with an untenable reality—because the addictive behavior removes us from the immediacy of experiencing it—then it follows that coming to terms with reality, and learning to accept it, is a fundamental part of recovery.

ACCEPTANCE OF SELF

My friend and colleague Alexander is gay. Growing up in the Mormon church, he was taught that his sexuality was a sin. In an effort to gain acceptance from God, his community, and his family, he did everything he could to try to change who he was, including voluntarily spending nine years in reparative therapy, which was aimed at "repairing" him into heterosexuality.

"At twenty-nine years old, I'd done all the things I was supposed to do to try to be 'good' according to the church, including trying to 'turn it off like a light switch'—it's a nifty little Mormon trick like they sing about in *The Book of Mormon* on Broadway," he told me, laughing. "But in the end, I was still attracted to men. I was still gay."

At a loss, he decided to take an international practicum

with his master's program and explore life outside his home state of Utah. He traveled across western Europe, Bulgaria, and Greece and was exposed to all kinds of cultural views on sexuality and the human body. He also began openly exploring sex with men, which he'd done before, but always privately and discreetly. When he returned from the trip, he tried to find a way to integrate his two worlds. He wanted to remain connected to and part of the church and his family, while also being true to himself.

Soon after he returned from his trip, Alexander was diagnosed with HIV. He immediately assumed this was his punishment for being sexually active with men—proof that what he was doing, and who he was, was a sin. "I believed I deserved it, that I'd done it to myself," he said.

To cope with his feelings of shame and rejection, Alexander started using drugs and alcohol for the first time, alongside his boyfriend, Jake, who was also HIV positive. Although he found deep connection and unconditional acceptance in that relationship, it was also destructive. They stayed together for four years, and during that time, Alexander's drug use worsened.

When Jake died by suicide in 2014, it sparked another awakening in Alexander. He realized he had to finally get sober (Jake had continued to suffer from addiction until he died), and he had to address the trauma he experienced in the church. Although he'd come so far, he still hadn't learned to truly accept himself as he was.

Now living in Southern California, he began to attend twelve-step meetings and found a group of other sober HIV-positive queer folks. What he learned from them was that he could find a God of his own understanding. "I learned I needed a Bigger God, one that accepted me exactly as I was." He was shocked to discover (as many people who grew up in a fundamentalist or evangelical religious community are) that this was even an option.

Through his recovery community and developing this relationship with a new "Bigger God," Alexander found true self-acceptance. "I joke that I didn't need to 'come out,' I needed to 'go in' and find the acceptance I was always searching for on the outside, inside."

PRACTICES FOR SELF-ACCEPTANCE

Alexander's story beautifully illustrates the four tools I believe we can all use to foster self-acceptance: finding "a Bigger God," which I've renamed "a Bigger Boat" to keep it secular (plus, who doesn't love a *Jaws* reference?), finding fellow travelers, loving-kindness meditation, and practicing solitude.

A BIGGER BOAT

Growing up in the Mormon church, Alexander learned a very specific set of beliefs that shaped his sense of self and what it meant to be good (and bad), right (and wrong), worthy (and unworthy) in the eyes of God. It wasn't until he began to have conversations outside of his community and travel the world that he learned he could choose his *own* beliefs and develop his *own* concept of God.

Whether you've had a religious upbringing or not, you've absorbed beliefs that shape your self-image and capacity for self-acceptance. And chances are, if you grew up in the West, particularly in America, you're accustomed to (and perhaps even numb to) a certain level of self-denigration and self-hatred. This is a complex phenomenon, but it can in part be tied to our Puritanical roots, which imprinted a morality around responsibility, hard work, and self-control into our culture and institutions. Add in hyper-individualism, late-stage capitalism, the endless social media scroll showing us everything we *could* be, everything we *could* have, and we're primed to believe any perceived failure or dissatisfaction is due to one thing: ourselves.

As for the Puritanical roots, although many of us wouldn't use this language, we still carry around something like the concept of "original sin," which says we were born bad and thus must continually repent in hopes of one day being good enough. And today, repentance has endless forms, from eating "clean" to chasing thinness to dutifully performing unpaid labor to optimizing productivity to hiding one's sexuality or political beliefs.

I remember the first time I became aware that my self-hatred stemmed in large part from the culture I grew up in. I'd heard a story about the Dalai Lama meeting with a group of Western Buddhist teachers in India in 1990. Sharon Salzberg, a world-renowned American Buddhist meditation teacher, reportedly stood up and asked the Dalai Lama, "What do you think of self-hatred?" She asked because it was something she battled with herself and had seen her American students struggle with consistently. The Dalai Lama turned to his translator again and again, trying to get clarification on the question, before finally looking to Sharon and replying, "Self-hatred? What is that?" As Sharon recounts, "This man, whom we all recognized as having a profound psychological and spiritual grasp of the human mind, found the concept of self-hatred incomprehensible, which made us aware of how many of us found it all but unavoidable."

Like Alexander being stunned when his friends in the recovery community told him he could form his own concept of God, Sharon (and later, I) was amazed to learn that self-hate wasn't a given. As it turned out, we could find a Bigger Boat.

What I mean by a Bigger Boat is a broader, more expansive, and ultimately loving container for our concept of self. One that not only accounts for mistakes, transgressions, and imperfections, but expects them and even encourages them, because all experiences (according to Buddhist philosophy, among others) are in service of our greater awakening.

Most of us don't question the underlying beliefs that inform our concept of self-worth. But once we're awakened to the idea that we *can* question them—which is what I'm giving you permission to do here—we can begin to examine them. When Alexander went looking for a Bigger God, he asked himself questions like: *Where did I get the idea that being gay was a sin? Who determined this, and what were they basing it on? Does this idea even make sense to me? What do other people believe? Why was the concept of God I learned in the church the only acceptable one? Who gets the final word on God? How did other queer people feel about their sexuality? What feels true about me, in my heart?*

When I was facing the reality of my addiction, I had to ask myself similar questions. *Where did I get the idea that addiction was some kind of moral failing? Why do I have to go to a church basement to talk about this? Why am I supposed to hide this part of me outside of those church basements? Why are we all lying to each other about our pain? Why are we so obsessed with alcohol, but so disgusted with people who get addicted to it? What feels true about me, in my heart?*

By asking these questions, I was beginning to create a Bigger Boat of self-acceptance. On a Bigger Boat, there's quite literally more *room:* room to question, to fuck up, to learn, to grow, to *breathe.* There's more room for you to take up space as exactly the person you are, instead of continuing to make yourself small, as so many of us (particularly women, people of color, LGBT+, or disabled folks) are taught to do in order to "get along."

If you feel ashamed in any way of who you are, especially about the parts of yourself that you can't control (even if other people say you can), such as your appearance, sexuality, gender, race, physical ability, socioeconomic status, traumatic experiences, family history, and so on, then you need to find a Bigger Boat. This also applies to things you may have chosen for yourself but others disapprove of or don't understand, like being single, not having children, or holding certain political beliefs. Bigger Boats make room for paradox, complexity, and the messy reality of being human.

Everyone who lives on a Bigger Boat understands this: True healing only ever comes from a place of love and acceptance, not self-recrimination and shame. We simply cannot hate ourselves into recovery. Often, when it comes to self-acceptance the problem isn't you. The problem is that the container you've been expected to live in is far too small. Sometimes you need a Bigger Boat.

Below are questions you can use to explore your beliefs about self, and hopefully move you closer to self-acceptance:

Do I accept myself, generally speaking?

If not, what parts of me do I believe are unacceptable?

Where did I learn that these things are unacceptable?

Am I willing to consider alternative, more open, loving, and accepting points of view?

What would a "Bigger Boat" of self-acceptance look like? Who would be on this boat? What would they believe? How would I feel being on it?

FINDING FELLOW TRAVELERS

When Alexander was diagnosed with HIV, a critical turning point for him in terms of self-acceptance was being introduced to Jake by a mutual friend at the university where Alexander was getting his master's degree. In their first interaction, Jake looked directly into Alexander's eyes, grabbed his hands, held them in his own, kissed them, and said, "I want you to know you are still worth loving and beautiful exactly as you are." While it sounds like a wildly intimate gesture for a first meeting, given the circumstances, it made sense. Jake knew exactly what Alexander was facing and feeling in that moment. At a time when self-acceptance seemed impossible for Alexander—when everyone around him only further confirmed his feelings of self-blame and hate—he desperately needed someone to tell him he was not only okay, but loved.

Interactions like these happen all the time in recovery spaces. People come in at their lowest point, isolated and choking on self-hate, convinced they're far beyond the pale of love and acceptance, oftentimes because they've been told exactly that. When they're welcomed in meetings or conversations with other sober people with open arms and told "nothing counts you out here," the relief and awe is immediate. Sometimes it's the first time in their entire life they've ever been received this way.

As important as it is to develop a sense of self-worth internally, it's impossible to do so in total isolation, or surrounded by people who will never understand what you're going through. This is why support groups exist for every possible cause: divorce, infertility, cancer, grief, parenting, and, of course, addiction. You name it, there's a group for it. Fellow travelers provide perspective that people who haven't been there can't; they relieve our sense of separateness and shame because we don't have to hide who we are with them; they love us as we learn to love ourselves.

My fellow travelers turned out to be other women in recovery. They reflected back to me the person I'd lost in my addiction: a strong, capable, dignified woman and mother. Because they saw me this way, I eventually did, too. The same thing happened for Alexander with Jake. It's possible for all of us, if we're willing to make the effort.

One of the gifts of modern technology is that finding fellow travelers isn't limited by geography. While IRL connections are always nice, we can also, and so easily, find connection online: Facebook groups, online support communities like TLC, virtual workshops and classes, Instagram accounts, Substack, Reddit threads; the options are nearly endless. With a little effort and intention, anyone with a phone and Wi-Fi can find their people. The catch is this: *You have to participate.* It's not enough to lurk in the comments, create a fake username, sit silently in a meeting, and expect people to reach out to you. You have to let yourself be known. It's okay to start slowly, but eventually you must dive in and raise your hand and use your voice. Oftentimes these virtual connections turn into IRL ones. I see it happen constantly in TLC, and it's happened for me so many times I can't count; some of my closest sober friends came from Instagram and Facebook groups—many I still have yet to meet in the flesh! This doesn't make their impact on my recovery any less meaningful.

I've included exercises and suggestions for how to connect with sober people or groups in chapter 6. You can also refer to the Resources section that begins on page 231.

LOVING-KINDNESS MEDITATION

Loving-kindness, or "metta"* meditation is one of the most powerful, science-backed forms of mindfulness meditation for generating feelings of compassion, goodwill, and warmth toward yourself and others. It involves repeating a set of simple phrases to wish you, and all beings, happiness, peace, health, and ease. The phrases go something like:

May I (you, we) be happy.
May I (you, we) be peaceful.
May I (you, we) be healthy.
May I (you, we) be at ease.

You begin by saying these phrases to yourself, and then extending them to other individuals, and then to all beings.

Research shows loving-kindness meditation has tangible benefits from increasing feelings of social connection, increasing positive emotions and decreasing negative emotions,

* "Metta" is a Pali word for benevolence, friendship, affection, and kindness.

activating empathy, and even healing physical ailments—all incredibly beneficial to anyone, but particularly to people in recovery, whose nervous systems and negative thought patterns are on overdrive.

Mindfulness is the practice of being present to the moment you're in (versus the future or past, where our attention usually is) and accepting the feelings, thoughts, and sensations that arise without judgment. In terms of self-acceptance, this is powerful because it helps us release the judgment and self-criticism that arise from the endless loop of stories we tell ourselves (based on the past or present) and instead ground ourselves in the now, where there is openness and possibility. As Sharon Salzberg, one of the foremost thought leaders on loving-kindness says, "Mindfulness enables us to cultivate a different quality of attention, one where we relate to what we see before us not just as an echo of the past or a foreshadowing of the future, but more as it is right now." This helps us build the "muscle" of self-acceptance, one breath at a time.

Speaking as someone who still struggles to meditate, I find loving-kindness meditation to be one of the most accessible forms of meditation because it follows a simple script, and there are innumerable resources and guides you can follow online and in meditation apps. Additionally, it's powerful in small doses; even five minutes can create a big shift.

SIMPLE LOVING-KINDNESS MEDITATION

1. Choose your phrases. Before you begin, choose three or four phrases that resonate with you from the list be-

low. These will be used throughout the meditation, the same phrases for each round. Write them down if you need to.

May I (you, we) be happy.
May I (you, we) be peaceful.
May I (you, we) be healthy.
May I (you, we) be at ease.
May I (you, we) feel safe.
May I (you, we) be free of pain.
May I (you, we) be free from harm.
May I (you, we) be free from suffering.

2. Get comfortable and focus on your breath. Find a quiet, comfortable place to sit. You can sit in any position that allows you to breathe deeply. Bring your attention to your breath by tuning in to the sensations of breathing in your body, such as the rise and fall of your chest and the sensation of air in your nose.

3. Repeat your chosen phrases to yourself. Go slowly, and repeat the cycle of your chosen phrases to yourself two times. For example: **May I be happy. May I be safe. May I be at ease.** *(Repeat). These can be said out loud or silently.*

4. Repeat your chosen phrases for someone close to you. Go slowly, and repeat the cycle of your chosen phrases to yourself two times. For example: **May you be happy. May you be safe. May you be at ease.** *(Repeat). These can be said out loud or silently.*

5. *Repeat your chosen phrases for someone who is neutral to you—someone for whom you have no negative or positive feelings. Go slowly, and repeat the cycle of your chosen phrases to yourself two times.* For example: **May you be happy. May you be safe. May you be at ease.** *(Repeat). These can be said out loud or silently.*

6. *Repeat your chosen phrases for someone you have negative feelings about. Go slowly, and repeat the cycle of your chosen phrases to yourself two times.* For example: **May you be happy. May you be safe. May you be at ease.** *(Repeat). These can be said out loud or silently.*

7. *Repeat your chosen phrases for all beings. Go slowly, and repeat the cycle of your chosen phrases to yourself two times.* For example: **May we be happy. May we be safe. May we be at ease.** *(Repeat). These can be said out loud or silently.*

When you've finished the meditation, take a few moments to consider any shifts in your breathing, emotional state, or the sensations in your body. If you don't feel any tangible shifts, **that is okay;** *this is a practice that takes time and is built like any muscle or skill.*

PRACTICE INTENTIONAL SOLITUDE

Our last tool for self-acceptance is the practice of intentional solitude. Oftentimes when people come into sobriety, myself included, they have very little sense of their own values and beliefs. This is partially due to the inherent disconnection from self that comes with substance use, but it's also a much broader problem of modern life. Our extreme focus on the external, most superficial aspects of self, combined with the ubiquity of smartphones, social media, 24/7 streaming, and all the other endless ways there are to distract ourselves, mean that we are almost never alone with our own thoughts or feelings. Cal Newport, bestselling author of *Deep Work* and professor of computer science at Georgetown University, labeled this phenomenon Solitude Deprivation: "[This generation] has lost their ability to process and make sense of their emotions, or to reflect on who they are and what really matters, or to build strong relationships, or even just allow their brains time to power down their critical social circuits, which are not meant to be used constantly." Cal determined this from decades of research on the influence of modern technology on our attention, and the focus and benefits of deep work and solitude on our productivity and well-being.

If you aren't feeling so great about yourself, it can be hard to spend time alone at first. But research shows that spending intentional time alone is incredibly beneficial for improving creativity and mental health, regulating mood, learning to satisfy our own needs, gaining important perspective, and increasing self-awareness. Like any other healthy relationship, our relationship with ourselves requires time, attention, and care. We need to learn who we are separate from the influence of others. You can't accept someone you don't know.

In my personal experience, embracing solitude has shown me that the world doesn't rest on my shoulders, that others can live just fine without me; it allows me to break the endless cycles of busyness and striving that I so easily fall into; most of all, it restores my perspective by reconnecting me to my heart and a broader, less self-centered perspective. It wasn't easy at first in sobriety, but eventually, the more I practiced it, the more I craved and appreciated it.

You don't need to go to a two-week silent retreat or disappear into the woods like Thoreau to practice solitude (although if you can, go for it!). Small increments, even ten minutes at a time, matter.

SIMPLE WAYS TO PRACTICE SOLITUDE

Put boundaries around your phone use. Our phones are the primary barrier to our solitude these days, so practice setting boundaries. Put off checking your phone for the first thirty minutes of the day (and wake up before your kids or significant other, if you have them). Instead of mindlessly scrolling, spend that time making coffee or tea, journaling for ten minutes, or sitting quietly with a pet or by yourself outside. You could also try putting your phone away an hour before bedtime and spend that hour winding down, meditating, doing some breathwork, or just *being.*

Meditate. Use the loving-kindness meditation or any other meditation.

Go for a walk without *your phone.* Or a hike, a bike ride, or simply sit anywhere outside. Whatever you do, don't bring your phone; look up and notice your surroundings.

People-watch in a park, at a beach, or in a museum.

Observe and wonder at what you see—and avoid the inclination to reach for your phone to document it and/or text people.

Make a date with yourself. *Set aside time for a date with just yourself, to do whatever you feel like doing. It could be as simple as taking an hour to get an ice cream, or an entire day where you browse your favorite bookstore and get lunch, take a long drive to a beautiful spot, or check into a hotel for a night and get room service. The point is to set aside the time and make it just for you—no work, no errand running, no bending to the needs and desires of others—for that period of time.*

Light a candle and watch the flame flicker. *This is a subtle form of meditation.*

Journal, draw, color, make a collage, organize your closet. *Simple acts done mindfully, and alone, count as solitude!*

ACCEPTING "EVERYTHING ELSE"

The sheer number of things we can't control in life (and thus, have to learn to accept) is absurd when you stop to think about it. Yet, we constantly deny or resist the limits of our control. Even the most evolved and wise among us are guilty of having, as Anne Lamott jokes, "tiny, tiny little control issues." Some more than others, to be sure (raises hand!). We want things to be a certain way: the way *we* think they should be. We want people to be a certain way: the way *we* think they should be. And we fight, tooth and nail, to try to shape the world in our own image. So much of personal development, self-help, and productivity culture is *built* on the promise of control—that if we just hustle harder, believe more, find the right pill/app/diet/whatever, think positive thoughts, and optimize every ounce of our time and energy, we can have it all. While it would take an entire other book to dismantle the harm the self-help industrial complex causes, all I want you to understand now is that when it comes to recovery, we must surrender; we must accept the reality of what's not in our control (beginning with the effect alcohol has on us). It's only in *surrendering* to that truth that we can begin to heal, grow, and reclaim our power. And it's only by accepting life as it is that we develop the capability and capacity to change it.

CHECK YES OR NO

I can't think of a better example of the ethos of acceptance than the twenty-five words of the Serenity Prayer. While the prayer was made famous in AA, it's generally attributed to American theologian Reinhold Niebuhr, though it's also been credited to many others, including Aristotle, Saint Augustine, and an ancient Sanskrit text:

> God, grant me the serenity to accept the things I cannot change, the courage to change the things I can, and the wisdom to know the difference.

(One need not reference God when reciting the prayer.)

I love the Serenity Prayer for its simplicity. No matter the situation, it asks us to answer one basic question:

Is this something I can control?

Answer 1: In my control = yes. Great, let's do something about it.

Answer 2: In my control = no. Okay, let's work on accepting it.

If you've realized something is not within your control, the next question is, of course, *how*. How do we accept reality when it feels too painful?

SEPARATE STORY FROM FACT

Remember the End of History Illusion from chapter 4? The finding that people tend to believe what they're experiencing right now is what they'll always experience, especially when they're in pain? This is one of the many cognitive distortions that happen when we believe the *stories* we tell ourselves rather than the objective facts.

For example, when I was newly sober, I thought my love life was over. Who would want to date someone who can't drink? What fun is it to be with someone who can never indulge, socialize with drinks, or have champagne at their wedding? I told myself all kinds of painful stories about what it meant that I couldn't drink alcohol and how limited, boring, and barren my love life would be. It broke my heart, and it kept me drinking.

We tell ourselves stories about all kinds of things: a breakup we didn't want, someone we love passing away, being passed up for a certain job or promotion, getting a scary health diagnosis; the scenarios are endless. We are meaning-making machines; it's what humans do. But our stories tend to cause us a lot of unnecessary suffering, and they can prevent us from being able to move forward.

The following exercise asks you to distinguish between fact and story. Although doing so won't necessarily alleviate the pain of the objective truth (for example, not being a drinker may in fact turn some people away!), we can at least challenge the stories we're telling ourselves and explore other possibilities (such as sobriety is actually appealing to *many* people).

Step 1: Consider the biggest challenge you face in sobriety. Write down all the thoughts and beliefs around this challenge and the consequences you fear will arise if you get sober.

For example, here's my list regarding sober dating:

I'm unattractive to potential partners.

Everyone wants to have drinks on a date.

Sober people are boring.

Nobody will love me sober.

I'll be single forever.

I'll die alone.

Step 2: Now, go back to each thought and write an "F" next to each one if it is a provable, objective fact, and an "S" next to it if it's a story we are telling ourselves, or an opinion.

Continuing with my dating example:

I'm unattractive to potential partners. F, but only because not everyone will be attracted to me; that is a fact of life for everyone.

Everyone wants to have drinks on a date. S. No proof.

Sober people are boring. S. When I thought about it, some of the most fun, interesting people I knew were sober.

Nobody will love me sober. S. No proof.
I'll be single forever. S. No proof.
I'll die alone. S. No proof.

As you do this exercise, you may find yourself working overtime to prove that some of the stories you've told yourself are indeed cold, hard truths. A great way to double-check your rationale is to share your list with someone you trust, ideally someone who can offer a broader perspective and doesn't share the same stories (that is, in this case, don't ask one of your hard-drinking friends).

So many of us go through life believing that our inner critic is the Ultimate Voice of Truth. Separating story from fact can alleviate some of the sting you feel about a particular situation and put you on a path toward acceptance.

"POWERLESS OVER" MANTRA

My friend Tammi keeps an always-in-progress list of things she cannot control. While certain things come on and off the list, two things are always at the top: alcohol and other people. When we were in the middle of the COVID pandemic, I heard her say probably one hundred times, "Well, Laura, today I'm reminding myself that I'm powerless over alcohol, other people, and pandemics."

It sounds almost too simple, but it works. Developing a basic, straightforward (and sometimes funny) daily reminder of what you cannot control is surprisingly effective. Try it.

PRACTICE 2: HONESTY

If I had to pick one practice for you to focus on in this chapter, it would be this. Honesty—learning to both hear and speak the truth—has been the most impactful part of my recovery. It's also become the litmus test of my own sobriety now that I haven't had a drink in eight years. If I'm being honest with myself and others, I'm sober. If I'm hiding or lying in some way, I'm not, and I have some work to do.

When we keep secrets, lie, or hide parts of ourselves away, we become disconnected from ourselves and others. And when we're disconnected, we're in danger, because we lose perspective, we feel isolated and alone, and shame creeps in. Remember the quote from Brené Brown about the three things shame needs to grow out of control in our lives: "secrecy, silence, and judgment." When we practice honesty, we eliminate two of the three.

The tricky part is that honesty isn't as straightforward as it sounds. We usually know when we're outright deceiving someone, like telling our partner we're not having an affair when we are, or stealing money from our company. It's the more subtle (but equally corrosive) forms of dishonesty that are harder to identify and overcome, like people-pleasing and all the myriad ways we "go along to get along" and "keep the peace" at home, work, and in friendships. We don't typically even see these things as forms of dishonesty (I didn't!) until it's pointed out to us.

The habit of lying or withholding, like any other coping mechanism, is almost always developed in childhood. I started lying as a young girl to try to control my dad's moods. If I acted happy and undemanding, it made things easier on him, and if he was in a good mood, I was more likely to get my needs met (or so my little brain told me). This dynamic was re-created in many of my relationships later in life. I'd present myself one way, but internally feel another—and it never worked out well for anyone. Most people lie not because they're terrible, malicious people who want to deceive and hurt others. Most of the time we lie because we're afraid of not getting what we want or losing what we have.

You may be wondering why honesty is so important. Most of us intuitively have a sense that lying isn't a great thing, but given how altering the truth can sometimes be (for instance, *If I'm honest about how I feel in my marriage, it might blow up my family*), isn't withholding sometimes a better option? How far do we go with it? And what if telling the truth actually harms others?

Honesty is important for many reasons, but all these reasons boil down to one thing: integrity. In Martha Beck's book *The Way of Integrity*, she makes a profound point: The word *integrity* comes from the Latin word *integer*, which means "intact." She says, "When a plane is in integrity, all its millions of parts work together smoothly and cooperatively. If it loses its integrity, it may stall, falter, or crash. There's no judgment here. Just physics."

Similarly, when we are out of integrity and our insides don't match our outsides, we can't operate or live well. As a result, we are chronically depleted, anxious, and overwhelmed from trying to catch up, repair, or clean up our lives and relationships. In short: We break down.

It's impossible to live with an addiction and be in integrity with oneself because addictions *require* dishonesty. We have to hide how much we drink, how often, and what happens when we're drunk, not to mention our pain and shame. We hide the real impact the alcohol has on us, even to ourselves.

This layer of dishonesty, though, is more symptomatic than causal. What I've noticed over the years is that, underneath the addiction, there's almost always a fundamental disconnect from the truth of one's own experience—a sort of inability to be with life as it is, or with ourselves as we are—that serves as the root of the pain. Whether we learn it by growing up inside a family where secrets are kept and problems aren't acknowledged, or by absorbing it from cultural messages about what's acceptable and what's not, or are outright told that our experiences aren't valid, or are inexplicably born this way, the result is the same: We learn to hide, to shapeshift, to lie. The resulting disconnection from the truth, or lack of integrity inside, is always painful; eventually it becomes intolerable, and we seek relief. For example, when my friend Sarah's mom and dad got divorced, her mom's "friend"—another woman—moved into their house. Throughout their entire childhood, Sarah and her sister were supposed to pretend like they didn't know that this woman, *who lived in their house,* was their mom's romantic partner. Sarah says the discomfort and unease created by the cognitive dissonance contributed heavily to her desire to numb, first through food and then alcohol. Keeping secrets, whether they're ours or someone else's, is corrosive to our psyche. This isn't speculation, it's science. There's a large body of research about the effect secrets have on our mental and physical health. Michael Slepian, a professor at Columbia Business School, whose entire body of work is researching the psychology of secrets and how they affect us, found that keeping secrets leads to measurable increases in anxiety, depression, loneliness, and low self-esteem. It turns out the old adage "We're only as sick as our secrets" holds a lot of scientific truth.

Most important, real connection is impossible without honesty, and we absolutely need authentic connection to recover. Again and again, it's been proven that recovery requires feeling safe enough to be honest about who we are and what we've gone through. This doesn't mean *everyone* we know needs to know *everything* about us, but it does mean we are no longer intentionally hiding significant parts of ourselves, especially from those closest to us. I was taught by other women in recovery that at least one person needs to know the truth about me, my past, and what I'm currently going through at all times. This doesn't mean one person needs to hold all that information—it can be spread across the circle of people I trust, including my partner, friends, my therapist, and so on. A simple question to ask yourself is *Does someone know this part of me / what I'm going through? If not, why?* If it's because you're ashamed, afraid of judgment, or otherwise feel an emotional burden, it's a solid tipoff that you need to talk about it.

Which brings us to how we decide whom we bring our secrets to. The general guideline is, if the information you're going to share with someone would cause them harm (like telling someone you've been having an affair with their wife for the past ten years) or place an unfair burden on them (like disclosing to your brother that you've been stealing money from the family business), then it's best not to share it with that person, but to share it with an outside, objective person instead, like a therapist, friend, or sponsor. The good news is, research shows that in instances like this, sharing secrets with an objective party provides significant relief for the secret keeper and improves their well-being, allowing them to move forward and heal. Of course, each situation needs to be evaluated individually, and we all need to rely on our instincts and intuition to decide what path is best, but a good rule of thumb is this: When in doubt, come clean with an outside, objective party first.

Below are three powerful methods for practicing honesty: boundary identification, numbing inventory, and the daily honesty scan.

BOUNDARY IDENTIFICATION

Developing healthy boundaries is a critical part of practicing honesty. Moreover, I would argue that all boundary issues are honesty issues. *Always saying* yes *when you mean* no? Boundary issue. *Withholding your true thoughts and feelings?* Boundary issue. *Representing yourself one way but feeling another?* Boundary issue. *Acting like you're okay with behavior you're not okay with?* Boundary issue.

I don't believe it's possible to recover from addiction or thrive in sobriety without developing healthy boundaries. My favorite definition of boundaries is from *The Book of Boundaries* by Melissa Urban:

> Boundaries are clear limits you establish around the ways you allow people to engage with you, so that you can keep yourself and your relationships safe and healthy.

If we cannot keep ourselves and our relationships safe and healthy, we're going to have a very hard time in life, sober or not.

The goal of this exercise is to identify when a boundary is needed. Doing so requires a willingness to be radically honest about what you feel, think, and need. Below I've listed three of the most common scenarios where boundaries are often lacking. From there, I've offered some of my favorite resources to help you learn more about boundaries and how to establish them.

SCENARIO I: YOU HAVE A RESENTMENT.

Resentments are one of the biggest indicators that a boundary needs to be set. Resentments are acute negative feelings that arise when we feel we are being mistreated, but often this resentment is due to not clearly communicating our needs.

Consider a person or situation that continually brings up feelings of resentment.

What is the story you tell yourself about this person or situation that causes these negative feelings to arise?

Describe your feelings (for example, I feel consistently unheard, run over, misunderstood) and how this person or situation is responsible for them.

Have you clearly and specifically stated how you feel to this person / group of people? Why, or why not?

What need(s) of yours are not being met in this scenario and what impact does this have on you?

SCENARIO 2: YOU FEEL CONSISTENTLY DEPLETED.

When what we're putting into a relationship or situation requires more energy than we get back, we're going to feel chronically exhausted, anxious, and depleted. Feeling this way is a great indicator that we need to set some boundaries.

Notice when you feel a pattern of exhaustion. It could be after having a conversation with someone, sitting through a meeting, going on a trip, exchanging text messages, or even anticipating such interactions.

Consider what it is that you specifically feel depleted by. It may be a certain conversation topic, lack of physical space in the interaction, questioning and judging your choices, or something more serious like racism, sexism, ableism, or homophobia.

What need(s) of yours are not being met in this scenario, and what impact does this have on you?

How could your needs be met?

SCENARIO 3: YOU FEEL ANGRY A LOT.

Before we go any further, if you're thinking to yourself, *Eh, I don't really get angry,* I'm going to call bullshit right away. *Everyone* gets angry, but for some people, like women and people of color, it's not acceptable or safe to express. Anger is a natural response to a boundary being broken. It's our body's way of saying, *Hey! Pay attention! Something needs protecting!* But when we ignore it or repress it and turn it inward on ourselves, we're left feeling hopeless and often ashamed.

When we don't demonize anger and allow it to flow freely (and channel it in healthy ways), it can be a huge asset, signaling to us that a boundary needs to be set.

Next time you notice the energy of anger arising inside you, observe your initial reaction to it. Do you try to push it down immediately, talk yourself out of it, or rationalize why you shouldn't be angry? Or do you explode on someone or something? Notice without judgment.

Next, ask yourself the following and journal your responses:

What boundary has been broken?

What needs to be protected?

What needs to be restored?

Note: If you are unfamiliar with acknowledging or expressing anger, these questions may be very difficult to answer at first.

NUMBING INVENTORY

Using the template below, document the history of your substance use (there are examples in the template below). Be thorough, but don't write long narratives. The point of this is to do an honest inventory of the past, what you used, when, and what consequences it had for you physically, emotionally, spiritually, and financially, if applicable.

This practice serves two purposes. First, it forces you to see—maybe for the first time—the full history of your numbing behaviors. While often difficult, this can be incredibly illuminating and helpful in reducing the discomfort of cognitive dissonance we so often have around our drinking. (Remember: The truth is ultimately freeing.) Second, and critically, it helps you make connections between challenging or painful periods in your life and your alcohol use. As you begin to understand the pain that drives your drinking, you'll find that you (probably, hopefully) have more compassion for yourself and why you sought to numb.

Important—before you begin: Doing this inventory may bring up difficult feelings. Plan for some aftercare following completion, such as a shower or bath, a walk, or a talk with someone you trust. If you have a history of unresolved serious trauma or PTSD, do not complete this exercise until you've consulted with a licensed mental health professional.

AGE/TIME-FRAME	SUBSTANCE/BEHAVIOR	FREQUENCY	REASON FOR BEHAVIOR	CONSE-QUENCES
5 years old	Food—bingeing	Whenever possible, daily	Feeling scared, uncomfortable, and insecure	N/A, don't remember
16–18 years old	Alcohol	Weekends	Wanting to belong, insecurity with boys	Sick, blackouts, grounded by parents
17–35	Food—restricting, bingeing, purging	Daily	Needing to numb feelings, wanting to be desired, hating my body	Obsession / one-track focus, severe unhappiness whenever above desired weight, difficulty with intimacy, more reliance on alcohol

21–28	Alcohol, cocaine	3–5 times/ week	Belonging, increasing physical dependence, needed for intimacy	Unwanted pregnancy, severe blackouts, drunk driving, compromised friendships, missing work because of hangovers
29–35	Alcohol, cocaine, Xanax	Daily (alcohol, Xanax); monthly (cocaine)	Physical dependency, inability to deal with painful emotions in marriage, shame and self-hatred for infidelity	Dissolution of marriage, financial problems including bankruptcy, putting daughter in danger, DUI, frequent blackouts and hangovers, panic attacks

Once you've completed the inventory, journal about the following:

How did it feel to write this out?

Did I learn anything new by doing this?

You may, at an appropriate time, consider sharing this inventory with someone else in recovery that you trust. You can either give it to them to read themselves, or read it out loud to them. The purpose is to share your experience with another, trusted person, so that you are no longer carrying the burden on your own. Feedback from that person is not required, and you can even ask that they do not give any, but instead simply receive your experience.

DAILY HONESTY SCAN

This last honesty practice is something you can do at any time to check in with yourself and see how you're feeling.

Instructions: Sit somewhere comfortable and private and spend ten minutes completing the following scan. Try to come up with three things for each category. Don't overthink the answers; write the first things that come to mind.

I am afraid / I fear:	I desire:
I resent:	I release:
I am grateful for:	I invite:

PRACTICE 3: CONNECTION

While our friends, family, and colleagues may want to be supportive of our sobriety and might be of great help, *we need people who understand our experience exactly.* I can't count the number of times I've met someone who's trying to get sober or has been sober for many years, but feels lonely, frustrated, and like they're missing the "magic" other sober folks talk about. When asked if they have sober friends or are close to other people in recovery, they say no. Oftentimes, they've put the burden on their partner, friends, or family to feel seen and supported and are understandably frustrated, because as well-intentioned as the people in our lives may be, they can't fill that specific need. In other words, it's possible to have healthy relationships and feel connected to people in your life while also being completely disconnected from your recovery.

CONNECTION CHECKLIST

1. *Do I have at least five phone numbers of people in recovery that I am comfortable using?* Note: Friends or family who are not in recovery do not count, even if those people "don't drink that much."
• If yes, great. List those people here and send each of them a check-in text, if you haven't recently.
• If no, what is your plan to make those connections? For example, join an online support group, attend a meetup, share in your support group that you're looking for connections. Make one small action toward this effort today.

2. *Do I have at least one voice-to-voice conversation (in person or on the phone—texting alone does not count) with someone in recovery every week?*
• If yes, great.
• If no, see question 1. Form a plan to establish a connection to at least one person you feel comfortable talking with on a weekly basis. Do this within the next week.

3. *Have I told my addiction/recovery story to at least one person or one group?*

• If yes, great.

• If yes, but it's been more than a year, make a plan to do so again within the next month.

• If no, make a plan to do that within the next two weeks by joining a group, raising your hand to speak in a support meeting, or connecting one-on-one with someone else in recovery. Note: You do not need to be sober yet to share your story! Oftentimes, sharing is a catalyst to staying sober.

4. *Do I have an established weekly routine for connection in recovery?* For example, attending a support meeting every Monday night, coffee with my sober friend on Sunday mornings, a daily email-based gratitude circle with other sober folks (my friend Tammi has been doing this for years), regular therapy, and so forth. Note, this must involve *other people in recovery;* journal writing by yourself, while great, does not count.

• If yes, great. Is it fulfilling? Is there an area where you need more support? What's the plan for creating that?

• If no, create a plan, be specific, and take action. For example, attending two meetings per week at specific times, scheduling a weekly coffee date with a sober friend, and so on.

We'll discuss the importance of connection in more detail in chapter 6.

PRACTICE 4: EMBODIMENT

The year my marriage ended, at the height of my drinking, I was teaching a yoga class and was demonstrating how to do Camel pose. The last part of the pose involves dropping the head back toward the ground, which can cause a pretty deep stretch in the throat. When I began to drop my head back, I immediately erupted in a fit of coughing, pulling me out of the pose. I tried again. Same thing, except now I felt like I was choking, too.

I also got strep throat three times that year. It's rare to get strep throat as an adult, but almost unheard of to get it multiple times in such a short period. During my last bout of strep, laid up in my bed feeling like absolute garbage, both from the strep and the alcohol withdrawals (being that sick was one of the few things that kept me from drinking then), I remembered something my original yoga teacher, David, had said during my first teacher training. We were practicing backbends and heart openers, and when we hit the same pose I'd taught in class, Camel, several people in the class including me began coughing. David, with his signature sense of humor, said, "Sounds like some of y'all need to stop telling so many lies!" We laughed, not totally getting what he was saying, but as we continued to practice, he went on to explain that the body doesn't lie. In fact, he said, our injuries, tension spots, aches and pains, posture, and gait often say a lot about our emotional lives.[*]

I filed this information away but kind of forgot about it until I was lying there in bed sick. As my throat burned raw

---

[*] This is not to say that all, or even most, injuries or illnesses have a strong emotional/mental component, or can be resolved through emotional/mental health.

and I could barely talk, I considered how many lies I was carrying: lies about my drinking, lies about my infidelity, lies about why I missed work again, lies about how scared I was, *lies, lies, lies*. It was all-consuming and exhausting keeping up with who knew what. I was on high alert all the time, afraid of being found out—to the point where every time my phone pinged with a text, I felt a jolt of panic in my gut. *Who's mad at me? What am I in trouble for now? Do they know?* I wondered if the two things—these lies and the strep plus recent coughing/choking fit while teaching yoga—were related. My intuition told me they were.

There's a saying in the field of psychosomatics (the field of psychology and bodywork that recognizes the mind-body connection), "Our issues live in our tissues." I've come to know the truth of this statement and have seen the healing that's possible when we address the mind-body connection through somatic therapies like breathwork, meditation, mindfulness, bodywork (massage and physical therapy), trauma-informed yoga, and the like.

One of my primary criticisms of conventional treatment programs like AA is the absence of acknowledgment of the body as a critical part of our recovery. To be fair, as I stated in chapter 1, back when AA was founded there was very little, if any, formal research or scientific understanding of trauma, neuroscience, or psychosomatics (though the yogis have understood it for centuries). Still, even now, the approach in many recovery programs remains "top down" and cerebral, using talk therapy and medication-based approaches. While we can get far with these types of treatments, research has proven that recovery that doesn't include "bottom up" approaches that address the body are incomplete—particularly in cases of trauma.

Trauma causes disruptions in the brain that lead a person to become hypervigilant, stuck in "fight, flight, or freeze" mode, unconsciously prepared for and looking for threats even when they're not there. It impairs one's ability to think clearly, feel a full range of emotions, and feel safe in their body. Given this reality, it's obvious why there's such a high correlation between trauma and addiction—living that way is scary, painful, and overwhelming. Who wouldn't seek relief? The good news is, real help is available. Below I've provided several practices you can explore—some of which you can do on your own, others that require a trained professional—to begin working on embodiment, healing the connection between body and mind.

I want to make clear that the benefits of embodiment aren't limited to people who have trauma. Everyone benefits from embodiment practices, even those who are physically unable to move their body because of paralysis, disease, or other reasons. If you're new to these practices, have unprocessed trauma, or any health concerns, please consult with your doctor or a mental health professional before doing any of these activities.

EMBODIMENT PRACTICES YOU CAN DO YOURSELF OR EASILY LEARN FROM A TEACHER OR APP:

- Mindfulness meditations (such as the loving-kindness meditation on page 116)
- Walking (try it without headphones on or carrying your phone)

- Hiking (try it without headphones on or carrying your phone)
- Yoga*
- Breathwork*
- Playing sports
- Progressive muscle relaxation*
- Sound healing*
- Chanting, singing
- Guided visualization*

*Might be best to first experience with a practitioner.

EMBODIMENT PRACTICES THAT REQUIRE PROFESSIONAL ASSISTANCE:

- Massage
- Physical therapy
- Hakomi
- Sensorimotor psychotherapy
- Neurosomatic therapy (NST)
- Somatic therapy
- Biofeedback
- Attuned touch
- Eye movement desensitization and reprocessing (EMDR)

PRACTICE 5: SERVICE

Service is dedicating time and energy to helping your fellow travelers. It's what "completes the circle" of our recovery because it connects us to the experience of others and extricates us from self-obsession and feelings of powerlessness. Anyone can be of service, anytime, whether you have one day of sober time or fifty years.

We often view service as a grand, sweeping gesture: volunteering for hours at a time, starting a nonprofit, raising thousands of dollars for a cause. Sometimes service does look like that, but more often it looks like the small, practical ways we show up for others in recovery.

Below are examples of service in recovery:

- Listening to another sober person share what's on their heart.
- Sharing your honest experience with another sober person.
- Calling another sober person and asking how they are.
- Texting another sober person and checking in on them.
- Showing up when you say you will for other sober folks.
- Speaking honestly in a support meeting.
- Reaching out to someone who's new in your support group and welcoming them.
- Sharing your experience with addiction and sobriety publicly, in an article, at an event, or on social media. (Not everyone is comfortable with this, understandably.)

The true magic of service is that we forget ourselves. When we are of service to others, we're pulled out of the ceaseless chatter of our own mean, punitive minds—the endless stories we are so often consumed by that keep us small and imprisoned. When we connect to others through service, we connect to their suffering, and we understand we are not alone—but more than that, we get perspective on our own problems.

As we grow in recovery, our capacity to serve grows. We

can hold more and therefore we can give more, whether it's through formal service or simply by being a living example of recovery.

· ·

As we close this chapter, remember, *please*, that the five practices of sobriety—acceptance, honesty, connection, embodiment, and service—are areas of growth, not something to perfect or achieve. Additionally, the exercises and practices I've outlined are only suggestions based on what I've found to be most powerful and effective for me and the people in my communities. Like everything else, the ultimate test here is your own experience. Be open to suggestions, but follow your own instincts. Seek out more information when you feel called, explore different modalities, and embrace a mindset of curiosity. The truth is, we *get* to do this work. Yes, it's hard. Yes, it will push you. Yes, it may turn you inside out. But if you've got even the most basic willingness and capacity to practice these things, this is an extraordinary gift you should not take for granted; many can't, or are unable, to take these steps either because they're so enslaved to addiction or they simply don't have the resources and support.

Above all, have *compassion*.

Compassion, compassion, compassion—more than you have ever allowed or imagined offering yourself.

6

YOU CAN'T DO IT ALONE.

I DESPISE THE IDEA OF BEING NEEDY. EVEN WRITING THE WORD *needy* makes me cringe.

I know I'm not alone. Even if you don't hate the idea of needing help as much as I do, I'm willing to bet asking for help doesn't come easily to you. I see people come up against this constantly when they're trying to get sober, and even well into sobriety.

And yet, society conditions us to glorify self-reliance. Look at what we idolize in modern culture: hyper-individualism, productivity, self-optimization, the appearance of perfection. Even the normal give-and-take of relationships is now often pathologized as codependence.

It was only after I got into recovery and had a lot of therapy that I uncovered the subconscious beliefs I had around being "needy." I was blind to how these beliefs influenced my life and all my relationships. The stories I told myself were:

Needing others is weak.
My value is in my strength and independence.
Being needy is gross and a turnoff.
Don't be a burden.

Any of those sound familiar? Here are some other greatest hits:

If it's going to be done right, it has to be done by me.
If you rely on others you're going to be let down.
Needing other people isn't safe.
Other people can't be trusted.
If people see who I really am (that is, my limits or failures), they'll reject me.
If I can't do it all, I'm a failure.
Other people's needs are more important than my own.
Someone else has it harder/worse, so buck up.
I should just be grateful for what I have.

How about those? I'm guessing you relate to more than a few.

The thing is, much of life is still manageable with the "go it alone" mentality. Sure, we may suffer from loneliness, and be chronically exhausted and resentful, but by and large, we can still muscle our way through a hell of a lot. We can take our insistence on self-reliance all the way to the grave, and many do.

Not in sobriety, though.

Sobriety is one of the rivers in life that we cannot cross alone.

It's way too hard. Far too deep.

Despite the fact that I still cringe at it, I've come to see the fact of my dependence on others as ultimately beautiful, edifying, and even strangely confirming of my inimitable power. Another paradox: It is only through reaching for another that we can discover the fullness of who we are. Or as David Whyte observed, "Without the understanding that we need a particular form of aid at every crucial threshold in our lives, and without the robust vulnerability in asking for that help, we cannot pass through the door that bars us from the next dispensation of our lives: we cannot birth ourselves."

Chances are, you know intellectually that you need help to get sober, but you don't *know-know* it yet—not in your heart. You're probably still trying to go it alone, either because you don't want the people around you to know how hard and dark it's been, you don't want to be a burden, or you think that it should be easier than it is. Maybe it's all three—it was for me. Many of us—no matter what our circumstances—have always *handled* shit. We've got a long list of evidence that proves how capable we are. We've prided ourselves on our ability to power through. And so we're convinced that if we just apply more of what's gotten us this far, something will click.

But it won't. I'm sorry.

And it's not because you're not all of those things, but because those things only ever get us so far. Sobriety is one of the few experiences in life that, if we fully embrace it, allows us to, as Richard Rohr says, "fall upward" into the second half of life: "Falling upward is a secret of the soul, known by not thinking about it or proving it but only by risking it—at least once. *And by allowing yourself to be led—at least once.* Those

who have allowed it know it's true, but only after the fact."
(Emphasis mine.)

The fact that we can't do it alone is what makes it so hard,
but it's also what makes it so worth it. Because what we get on
the other side is the experience of *actually* being known—of
being seen. We get what we've been searching for all along:
We get love.

> **QUESTIONS:**
>
> *What stories do I tell myself about depending on others,
> being needy, and/or asking for help? Where did these
> stories and beliefs come from?*
>
> *Am I trying to do sobriety alone? If so, why? Is it work-
> ing for me?*

JUST ANOTHER NOODLE

In my early days of attempting sobriety, I was talking to another sober woman and relaying how I'd spent the entire week
anticipating an office happy hour: playing out hypothetical
conversations, what I'd say if various people asked me if I
wanted to drink, what my response would be if they asked
why I wasn't drinking, whether to show up early or late, the
exact words I'd use to order a Diet Coke (or should it be a
seltzer and lime?), and on and on. After I shared all my insane
mental gymnastics with her, I looked at her and said, "I mean,
who *does* that?" She laughed and replied, "Laura, you're just
another noodle in the soup."

Aside from being funny, I found the sentiment so comforting. She didn't think I was crazy or dramatic or weird or annoying or exhausting or anything else. She'd done the same things herself, and so had everyone else she knew in sobriety. Other people might've thought it weird, but she didn't because my thing was her thing, too. *I was just another noodle in the soup.* What a relief.

We know now that shame is highly correlated with depression, suicide, eating disorders, and as we've discussed, addiction. We also know shame can't survive in empathy-filled light. Meaning, shame dies when we bring our secrets to light, when we share our secrets with others, and when those secrets are received with empathy.

Empathy is the ability to understand and share the feelings of another. There are a lot of empathetic people in the world, but often, and especially when it comes to addiction, we find them lacking. We've all experienced this, no doubt, even from well-meaning family and friends who love us but simply cannot understand why we would put ourselves and them through such hell with our drinking. Even if they genuinely want to get it, they can't, and their misunderstanding and judgment only further the spiral of shame and isolation we feel.

Which is why, to truly recover, we don't only need other people—*we need our people; we need other noodles.*

We need people who know *exactly* what it's like to lose yourself in an addiction, to go against your own integrity, to both love something and know it's ruining your life, to feel those same gradients of despair, shame, regret, and fear. We need people who know all the invisible ways this thing burns.

Without that level of understanding, we won't get the empathy we need, and without the empathy, we can't overcome the shame, and if we don't overcome the shame, we can't heal.

But even beyond the shared experience of addiction, we need people who share our background and formative experiences.

I would never have gotten sober if not for hearing other mothers talk about the shame of being a mother who drank. Similarly, many of the men I know in recovery find that they need to connect with other men and have the conversations only they can have together. These basic differences in experience have been recognized in recovery programs for some time now; you'll often see closed men's and women's meetings offered in AA, for example. But beyond gender, discussion of the impact of other aspects of identity or experience on one's addiction and sobriety, such as race, social class/socioeconomic status, or sexual orientation are often categorized as "outside issues," meaning they're too "controversial," "political," or outside of one's relationship with God through sobriety, and thus don't belong in meetings.

Remember Chris from Texas? He shared with me that on several occasions in support meetings, when he talked about an experience with racism during a share and how it was affecting his sobriety, he was pulled aside afterward and told *We don't talk about that here. That's an outside issue,* even though his shares were sobriety focused. Chris says it wasn't until he reached nearly twenty years of sobriety and got involved in a new recovery community, where closed BIPOC meetings were offered (meaning only people of color are allowed to attend), that he felt like he could speak honestly and get the support and understanding he so desperately craved and needed. Twenty years. And in that time, Chris had not only been a part of various recovery communities, he'd worked inside them as a mental health counselor. He'd spent thousands of hours both facilitating and participating in these communities and never felt truly at home until he could connect with other people of color in a closed space. The murder of George Floyd was a tipping point for him, after which he decided that "going forward, I refuse to leave the heaviest part of me at the door. And if I'm asked to, I know it's not a place for me."

Similarly, my friend and colleague Anthony shared that having closed queer-focused sobriety meetings has been a game changer for his sobriety because the only way he knew how to meet people in the queer community or be intimate was through alcohol. "When I came out, it was always about 'Where are we doing brunch?' or 'Which bar are we going to tonight and where are we pre-gaming?' or 'Let's get drinks' if you're going on a date—*everything* revolved around drinking."

Spending time in sober spaces with other queer people has been healing in every way, Anthony says. He feels more alive in his queer identity than he ever did when drinking, and as a meeting leader, he has been able to witness an incredible level of healing because of the shared space they've built. "A lot of people have trauma from being dismissed by their families, or being told by their church that they no longer belonged and were going to hell, and that, of course, is so intertwined with drinking. This is stuff only we really understand."

. .

A common refrain in both the culture at large and in recovery spaces is "Let's focus on our similarities and not our differences." While it's important to connect over shared experiences, that connection can happen in good faith only when our differences and the *impact* of those differences—including the prejudice, oppression, and discrimination that have occurred because of them—have (at minimum) been acknowledged. For recovery to truly be possible for everyone, we need consistent and conscious efforts to acknowledge, represent, and make space for experiences that are not white, straight, able-bodied, and cisgender.

Thankfully, we are beginning to see this happen, with the recent proliferation of online support groups and new models for recovery. In The Luckiest Club, we have BIPOC, queer-focused, women's, and men's meetings. Similar offerings are available in groups such as Monument, She Recovers, Reframe, and more. A full list of groups are available in the Resources on page 231.

What I want you to take away is twofold: Anything you believe is too weird, awkward, embarrassing, or wrong about you when it comes to drinking (or sobriety) is nothing but . . . totally normal. There is no weird anymore. Not to us, anyway. To us, you're just another noodle in the soup (this is now an actual saying we use in TLC all the time). Which is why we need one another. Second, there's a place for you, no matter who you are. You do not need, as Chris says, *to leave the heaviest parts of you at the door.* Not anymore. All of you is welcome— maybe not everywhere—but definitely here.

QUESTIONS:

What parts of my alcohol use carry the most shame?
(For example: *being a mother who drank.*)

What aspects of my life experience or identity do I need to feel safe and free to talk about in order to feel truly supported and seen in my recovery?

If I could imagine my ideal support community, what would it look like? What would be offered? What kinds of people would be there?

What are three actions I can take today to connect with this type of support? (Refer to the Resources on page 231 if helpful.)

MIDWIVES AND MIRRORS

About six months before I finally got sober, I went to a party in Washington, D.C. It was organized by one of my former colleagues from an agency we used to work at together, for all the current and former employees who had kept in touch.

The period in my life when I'd worked at this agency was something of a golden time. When I started there in 2006, I'd just married but didn't yet have the responsibility of being a parent, or having a mortgage, or feeling like I was supposed to have anything figured out. Most of us were in the same place: that bubble of time between your late twenties and early thirties where everything feels wide open, your body is resilient, and there's always enough energy, time, and money—even when there isn't. We fully embraced the work hard/play hard ethos. Our colleagues were also our best friends and sometimes felt more like family than our actual families. We loved one another, annoyed one another, confided in one another, learned from one another, built our résumés together, and kept one another's secrets. We had crushes, made alliances, bonded under deadlines, and accumulated a million inside jokes. And, of course, there was booze everywhere: after work, at parties, on weekends, at client dinners, during client trips, and in the actual office.

My own drinking started to turn the corner during those years, but it was still fun enough, often enough, that I could ignore it. By the time we met up for the reunion party, though, everything was different. I was separated from my husband, had been a mother for five years, and any innocence I'd had around my drinking was long gone. I knew I had to get sober—had known it for nearly a year, since my brother's wedding—but I was still heartbroken about it, and so stuck.

When people started to talk about coming together for a reunion, I was seized with nostalgia. I knew there was no way I could go and stay sober; I didn't even want to try. I wanted to show up and, for a couple of hours, feel what it was like to be the me from back then: to feel free and light and young, like everything was still possible, instead of carrying around the weight of what my life had become. I wanted to laugh and be stupid and silly and, God, I wanted some of that innocence back. I wanted to be seen like I used to be seen—as fun, smart, ebullient Laura—before I'd started to scare and disappoint and hurt people, before I became the one with A Problem. And I knew these friends would see me that way because they hadn't been close enough in recent years to see the truth. I knew I was fooling myself. I knew I'd have to face reality the next day. But I wanted a reprieve so desperately.

Still, I told myself I wouldn't drink at the party while knowing full well I would. Even on the train ride down to D.C., I pretended like I wasn't going to, to keep my guilt and anxiety at bay. I even told a couple of people that I was closest to in the group that I wasn't drinking anymore but left out the details of why.

I went to a friend's house before the party so we could Uber in together, and we had a few vodka sodas. When we got there, it was exactly as I expected. It was like stepping into a time machine, and it felt good—so achingly good—to feel *normal* again. But in the background of every interaction, every hello and hug and catch-up exchange, the truth was whispering in my ear. *You're lying. You're a fraud. This is all a big charade.* As the night went on, it grew louder and louder, and although I kept drinking, after a while I couldn't drown it out.

I went outside to get some air and a woman named Amy, whom I'd worked with but not closely—she was sort of an enigma at the agency, on the senior account team, a mother, tall and exotic looking, and mysteriously absent at all the happy hours—was sitting at a picnic table with her fiancé. I felt strangely drawn to her and walked over, sat down, and asked if I could bum a cigarette. We were friends on Facebook, and I had followed her story of meeting her now fiancé. It was a sweet story I clung to perhaps a little too tightly, since, like me, she'd also been a divorced, single mom. Something about the way she talked about her fiancé and their connection struck me as genuine and hopeful. I told them this and congratulated them on their engagement.

We quickly fell into easy conversation and I felt compelled to tell her what was going on with me, with the drinking, trying to get sober.

"I am trying to get sober and—" I started.

She stopped me, put down her Diet Coke, took my hands with both of hers, and looked straight into my face. "I know. I knew! I could tell." She smiled at me with such knowing kindness my throat swelled.

"*How?*"

"I just knew. We can smell each other," she said, and laughed. "Here, I have something for you," she said, as she let go of my hands and grabbed her purse from beside her on the bench and fished out her wallet. She opened it up, unzipped the change pocket, pulled out a big coin, placed it in my palm, then laid her palm over it. I knew what it was: a sobriety chip. It was heavy and cool in my hand.

"This is for you. It's yours now," she said, wrapping my fingers around it.

I opened my hand and looked at it. In the middle it read "XVII." Seventeen years of sobriety.

"Oh my god. Seven*teen*? You're my hero," I said.

"Yep, I just got it. Take it."

I jumped up from my seat to hug her. "Thank you," I said

into her thick, long black hair that smelled like cigarette smoke and shampoo. "Thank you."

As I put the heavy coin in my back pocket I told her I was going to keep it forever. I was still in a bit of shock, but I noticed all my anxiety was gone. Even though I'd had a bunch of drinks, I couldn't feel the buzz of the alcohol anymore, just a shimmering knowing that I would, at some point in the near future, get sober for good. I had a surety I hadn't felt before, but also something else. When I looked into Amy's face, saw her joking with her fiancé, sipping from her drink and smoking another cigarette, smiling bright and clear and rolling her head back as she laughed with her whole body, blowing the smoke up toward the sky.

I felt hope.

A different kind of hope, though: hope for sobriety. Hope for the future, instead of wishing I could go back to the past.

I stayed at the table with them for a long time, asking questions about how she did it, sharing parts of my story, talking to her fiancé about how he felt about her sobriety, and when they left I hugged them both like I'd known them forever. We promised to keep in touch. I thanked her again, and she knew where the gratitude came from—from the deepest part of me. She knew what I'd been given, because she'd been given the same thing along the way, from those who went before her.

I navigated the rest of the party differently, like I had the world's best secret in my pocket. I felt new, more solid, as if so many disparate pieces of myself that had been floating around, snagging and getting stuck, unsure where to tether or how, had collected in my center and snapped into place. I knew I was going to make it.

· ·

I look at that exchange with Amy as a "midwife" experience. We often think of midwives as people who assist a mother in giving birth, but there's another, broader definition: a person or thing that helps to bring something into being or assists its development.

Helps bring something into being or assists in its development.

That's what Amy did that night. She brought a piece of me—*sober me, the me I could be, if I pushed off*—into being. When she looked at me and grabbed my hands, even knowing I was still drinking, she had no doubt. She knew what was possible for me—she saw it as already done, already realized—and because she did, I could glimpse it, too. More than that, I could already feel it inside of me; the alchemy had happened.

This is one of the hundreds of similar stories that I have now. I hear this kind of thing regularly from other sober people, so much so that I'm not even surprised anymore. The right person at the right time who says the right thing. Midwives for whom we are becoming.

In my experience, once you set even the smallest intention toward change, these people begin to show up. As the saying goes, "When the student is ready, the teacher appears." Even if you don't *feel* ready, your soul probably is—and that's what matters. Souls communicate with other souls on a subterranean level. And sobriety is no less miraculous than the birth of a child. Midwives know the tactical, practical aspects of giving birth *and* they know the ineffable, intuitive parts that can't be found in a library of books. The same goes for sobriety.

While some people will serve as midwives in your recovery, others will be mirrors. Most of us have such incredibly distorted views of ourselves—views that were shaped long before we began drinking—because we've never had a kind, compassionate mirror to reflect us back to ourselves. Add the insult of addiction into the mix and the distortion only becomes worse.

Mirrors are people who reflect our true selves back to us, the person we are behind all the drinking and trauma and bad behavior and shame and mistakes. We need mirrors to reflect this back to us when we cannot do so ourselves.

The minute I began to meet other sober people, I started to see pieces of who I *really* was reflected back to me—from Grant, who told me I was not bad, but sick, to the woman in that first meeting who told me to *push off from here,* to the other mother who told me that who I was when I was drinking wasn't who I was, and on down the line. It took thousands of interactions over many years, but eventually I stepped into the dignity they reflected back to me.

As a result, I've been able to be a mirror for others, like my friend Karla, who called me several years ago after a two-day blackout wherein she'd been caring for her kids and taking them to and from school. She was alone, afraid, and ashamed of these episodes, which had put a massive strain on her marriage and job. Through my writings and mutual friends, we'd become acquainted, and she reached out after coming to from her blackout. I drove to her house, contacted her husband and family, and helped get her placed into inpatient rehab—all without any judgment, only love and compassion, because I had been there. As she navigated the inevitable shame spirals of those days before going to rehab, I was able to reflect back to her what I knew to be truest about her: that she was a loving mom, daughter, and wife; a wildly talented artist; and a gorgeous soul—not what she felt because of the addiction, or what some of the people in her life were telling her at the time. I was able to do this only because I had my own mirrors. And I wasn't just paying her lip service to get her to calm down; my reflection of her was what I *knew* to be the truth.

To be clear, not every sober person you meet will be a positive reflection for you. There are all kinds of people in recovery, and not all of them are well-meaning or healthy. But by and large, my experience has been exceedingly positive *when* I made the effort to reach out and put the work in to connect.

If you look around your life right now and see only negative reflections of who you are, if the people closest to you—your family, your friends—don't support you in your sobriety and don't reflect back a positive, benevolent version of you, you're not alone. In psychology, this behavior is known as "the crab effect," or "the crab mentality," named for the behavior of crabs in a bucket: When one tries to escape, the other crabs immediately try to pull it back in. Humans have similar tendencies—we will often try to undermine and halt the progress of other, better-performing peers. The thinking goes something like "If I can't have it, you can't either."

I hear stories like this all the time, whether it's someone's spouse ordering them their favorite drink at dinner "by accident," friends peer-pressuring someone to drink or casually mentioning how fun they used to be when they were drinking, or a mother-in-law leaving behind bottles of wine after the birthday party, even though they were asked not to.

These people can't be mirrors for you no matter how badly you want them to be; they can only be crabs. Don't exert any more energy trying to get their permission to leave the bucket. Set about finding the mirrors instead. We're here, ready to show you who you are.

QUESTIONS:

Are there people in my life who are behaving like "crabs"?

Am I willing to let go of the need for their support?

Do I have positive "mirrors" in my life? Who are they? If not, am I willing to find them?

Have I had the experience of a midwife "magically" appearing to support me in getting and staying sober?

IT TAKES A VILLAGE BUT IT STARTS WITH ONE

Recently, someone posted the following in a sobriety Facebook group I follow:

Hi all. I don't want to join AA or a group, but I'd like someone to text me when I want to drink and remind me why it's not a good idea. Is anyone willing to do that?

I see posts and hear people say things like this all the time and I get it, of course, but I'll be blunt: A text buddy is never gonna be enough. That's like trying to put out a forest fire with a water gun. *It's not even close to enough.* You don't need one person to text when you want to drink, you need ten of them for when the first nine don't answer, and then another ten for backup. You need people in real life, people on screens, people in support rooms, people who've already gone all the places you'll go, people who are walking alongside you, amateurs and professionals. You need people you can reach out to, yes, but you also need people who can sense a disturbance in the force before you even know it's there and will ask things like *You've been quiet, how's it going? You don't seem like yourself lately, are you okay? Have you been to a meeting lately? How's your heart?*

We need a village of people to get and stay sober, like we need a village of people to raise kids. Sobriety—and life—are too complicated, and it's *way* too much to pin on one person. And besides, we don't just want to *not drink*—we want to actually live, right? I have learned as much about the bright side of living—the fun, the joy, the laughter, the playfulness— from being around other sober people as I have about how to handle the hard, heavy stuff.

This is not to say that we must shape our entire lives around sober people. But we do need to decenter drinking in our lives, and that might mean changing up the people we spend time with. While that can be a painful transition, in the end, it's freeing and fulfilling. Who wants to always feel like they're "other"? No one. Who wants to feel like they're always missing some essential part of the experience because they're not partaking? No one. So many of the people and things I thought were fun when I was drinking aren't remotely fun at all. I drank to *make* them fun. I've had far more fun in sobriety than I ever had drinking, but it required submitting myself to a period of uncertainty, change, and loneliness. In that space, new people came in. All of them mirrors.

I recently heard a woman share that she'd just achieved ten years of sobriety, and it wasn't until this past year—her ninth year—that she felt connected and unashamed about her sobriety. She said when she got sober, the only thing she knew of was AA. There were no podcasts, no sober Instagram accounts, and only a few recovery memoirs, all written from a twelve-step perspective. She did get sober in AA and expressed boundless gratitude for the program and the people in it—*and*, she said, because anonymity was stressed—she always felt like she was living in two worlds: the private one where she was able to talk about this critical part of her life, and the public one, where nobody knew about it. As so many new programs, different narratives, and public voices have emerged around sobriety, things changed for her. "Something in me was always ashamed because I was carrying a secret—that it was *supposed* to be a secret—because it was too ugly to share out loud," she said. "For the first time now, at *ten* years sober, I am proud of it. Because I'm connected to other people—women and mothers like me, specifically—who are proud of it, too, and talk about it openly." It takes a village.

Many people feel overwhelmed (and understandably sad and scared) by the idea of changing their social circles and creating this village I'm talking about. But I always remind them it only ever starts with one. One person is all you need to begin. One midwife, one mirror, one noodle, is all it takes.

So, let's talk about how you can go about finding them. But before I start, I want to issue some important warnings.

First: If you are in need of detox or inpatient treatment, please call your doctor, dial 911, or check yourself into an ER immediately. Alcohol withdrawal can be fatal. The tips below are not meant to provide help in the case of life-threatening emergency or need for detox.

WAYS TO FIND SOBER SUPPORT

ONLINE

• Do a hashtag search on Instagram (or TikTok, I hear) for #sober, #soberlife, or #wearetheluckiest and browse around. See if there's anyone you're drawn to, spend some time on their feed, interact with their content, and send a direct message to them if it feels right.

• Search Facebook for sober groups—there are thousands of them now (ones I recommend are included in the Resources on page 231). You can search by location, identity, and affinity group. Typically, you'll be asked to answer a few questions before joining, but otherwise, it's super easy. Spend time observing other members and, most important, *participate*. If you're worried about privacy, either create a separate Facebook account for this purpose, or share anonymously as a "Group Member" (a new feature in Facebook as of summer 2022).

• Search for "online sobriety support groups" and explore. Some programs are free, some are paid, and many offer scholarships. (The Luckiest Club does, no questions asked.) Join and attend meetings, participate in their platforms, and make an honest effort to reach out to other members.

• Share in online meetings. There are a lot of people in TLC meetings who join but never turn their camera on and never share—for months and years at a time. While everyone has to go through the process of getting comfortable sharing (it's hard!), I've yet to find anyone who has been successful in sobriety or feels connected to others by staying silent. Yes, it's *hard* to open your mouth, but we've all had to jump off that cliff at some point, and the only way to make it easier is to do it! Take your time, but don't wait too long.

• Check out Reddit for sober threads. There are several strong ones, such as r/stopdrinking.

Whatever online methods you choose, the key is to *not* remain an anonymous lurker. If you make an honest effort, you'll be amazed at the generosity and goodwill people show.

WARNINGS AND GUIDELINES FOR ONLINE INTERACTIONS:

• Seeking out only online connections can become a way to hide, especially if you're seeking out "influencers" or other people with whom you don't form an actual one-on-one relationship that moves beyond social media. Beware of this. A genuine connection provides mutual support.

• Make sure you practice discernment and safety— there are a lot of great people out there, but also a lot of weirdos. Don't give away sensitive personal information without doing the appropriate background work. If you're unsure, ask for an outside opinion.

• Beware of anyone who is trying to sell you something, whether it's coaching, a course (even a "free" one), or a program of any kind. There are a lot of "sobriety coaches" out there these days. Some are credentialed, many are not (there are no standards or requirements to be a coach—anyone can slap that label on themselves at any time). If coaching is something you're interested in, that's fine, but be sure to do your research. Ask about qualifications, be sure the person has solid sobriety (time isn't everything, but I would be wary of working with someone who has less than a couple of years) and check at least three references before you agree to anything.

• Similarly, beware of sponsored ads for treatment centers. Unfortunately, the addiction treatment industry is rife with fraud and malpractice. A great source for reliable treatment centers is lovefirst.net/resources.

• If you're part of an online group, specifically *ask for support.* Tell people you're looking for new connections, and include relevant details about: your location (general), roles or identities (for example, parent, queer, BIPOC, over fifty) that are important to you, and so on.

Be consistent and don't give up. Sometimes it takes a few tries and some trial and error to find a person or group that feels right. This is normal and should be expected. Stay open, positive, and curious.

IRL

• *Look at your existing network.* Chances are, you probably already know people in recovery. They may be colleagues (Salesforce has a sober support group called Soberforce), friends or acquaintances from high school, people you used to work with, or your neighbors. Do a little thinking and you may realize you're connected to more sober folks than you know—either directly, or through others. I've been contacted by friends of friends, cousins of friends from high school, people who know someone I used to work with, and so on. It's never weird and it's always welcome. While I may not have space to spend time with everyone myself, I am always happy to refer them to people or resources.

• *Sports or fitness leagues.* While some sports leagues have a strong "booze" component, there are often sober factions within them. I've found sober communities within yoga, CrossFit, Peloton, volleyball, and more. If there's an activity you like or something you want to try, this can be a cool way to do that thing while making sober connections. The Phoenix is a sobriety-focused fitness community that has gyms and programs in more than twenty states as of this writing, as well as online events.

• *Volunteer groups.* Soup kitchens, shelters, food banks, and most other kinds of volunteer groups don't involve alcohol on the "job." These kinds of groups can be a safe, fulfilling way to meet people in a non-boozy environment, and you may find out that some of them are sober.

• *Sober bars.* Yes, these now exist. Chris from Texas opened Sans Bar, a sober connection space in Austin, Texas, in 2017, and he frequently hosts sober events throughout the United States. In recent years, this movement has started to expand. Awake in Denver, On the Other Side in Illinois, Listen Bar in NYC, and Getaway in Brooklyn are all new spaces dedicated to creating sober social experiences.

• *IRL support groups.* There are many. Look them up, show up, and see what you find.

• *Search for sober events.* A simple search for "Sober events near me" will yield dozens of results, if not more, depending on where you live. You may have to drive a bit, but if you find that first connection, it's worth every mile.

A full list of social media accounts and online sober groups is available in the Resources on page 231.

· ·

Eight years ago, when I got sober, most of these opportunities didn't exist. I'm thrilled there is so much more available now, and that I can say with confidence that you can find what you need if you make an honest effort.

But you've got to make an honest effort.

As much as I wished the right people would magically appear at my front door when I needed them, they never did. I had to go out into the world and push against what was comfortable, and so will you. When you do, the world will begin to open itself up to you, and the midwives, mirrors, and noodles will appear. Recognize them when they do, and walk on.

1

ONLY YOU CAN DO IT.

ON A SWELTERING SUNDAY AFTERNOON IN JULY 2014, NAUSEOUS from the heat and a hangover, I strapped a five-year-old Alma into her car seat and trekked into Boston to go to an author event with Elizabeth Gilbert. I nearly talked myself out of making the drive, which could easily turn into an hour or more each way with summer beach traffic, but I knew I'd hate myself for not going on account of a hangover. It was a too-old excuse, and I'd wanted to see Liz speak for years.

It had been a full year, almost to the date, from my brother's wedding when I'd left Alma in the hotel room. A year since I had gone to my first sobriety meeting. A year since I started to face my drinking. Since then, I'd begun writing about my trials, telling the truth for the first time on the page, publishing blog posts every so often and sending them out to my friends and family or posting them to Facebook when I felt brave. I was barely giving myself permission to think of myself as a writer and imagine that I may have it in me to write a book—my long-held, mostly private dream. It made no sense; no part of my life was pointing toward this at the time, not my education, job experience, or habits (aside from always being a voracious reader). But when I was able to push through the doubt and impostor syndrome and write, I felt something happening inside me, an uprush of energy and urgent momentum, a sense of being outside of time. It was one of the few things that made me forget myself.

But I was still drinking. Alma and I were living in a tiny one-bedroom apartment with our dog, sharing a bed, and every couple of weeks I'd drink a few bottles of wine alone and take several Ambien, burning down all the sober momentum I'd built up. I was still looking for that third door. I was still waiting for some kind of rescue from the outside—a strike of lightning, a boyfriend, something—to make it easier. I was sure a time would come when it would just be *easier*.

Mercifully, the book event was in a cold, dark theater. When the doors opened, I scrambled to the front to get us good seats. I wanted to be as close as possible but also hoped being right by the stage would keep Alma entertained and quiet.

When Liz walked out, I stood up to clap and my legs turned to Jell-O. I was overwhelmed by a tidal wave of energy. I'd felt the same wave before when I'd gone to other author events or read memoirs by other women over the years, though never quite so strongly. It was more than a tug of envy; this was guttural.

When I looked at her hands holding her book as she was

reading to us, I felt a desperate desire to grab it, hold it in *my* hands, and hear the soft sandpaper scratch of the paper on *my* fingers as I flipped the pages.

I wanted the bright lights shining in *my* eyes.

I wanted to stand on the hardwood of the stage in my boots and feel *my* body in space, behind a podium, looking out at a sea of people.

I wanted to laugh and smile and answer questions and look directly into people's faces and share *my* work, *my* words.

I wanted all of it. Even though it was worlds away from my reality. I wanted it so bad.

After she read from her book, Liz took questions from the audience, and someone asked her how she overcomes writer's block. She answered by saying that she didn't believe in writer's block as an isolated force independent from the rest of our lives. Often, when we say we have "writer's block," it means there is some area of our lives that we need to face or address, and it's *that* thing that's blocking us. She started listing off examples:

A toxic relationship
An unaddressed health issue
A soul-sucking job
Unprocessed trauma
An addiction
Living somewhere you hate
Hiding your sexuality

She continued on, but my heart snagged when she said it. *Addiction*. Right there in the middle of all the other things she listed, she named my thing, as if it wasn't any bigger than the rest, as if it was just another experience people have in life.

Something jelled. I knew my drinking had to stop—that wasn't news. But hearing her name my thing right then, as I was literally sitting inside a living, breathing manifestation of my dream, *hungover,* I felt the plainness of it all for the first time.

It was either drinking or this. Alcohol or my dream. The two would never coexist.

It wasn't only that it would be *harder* to become an author if I kept drinking, or that it would take a little *longer*—it straight up wouldn't happen.

I had to stop fucking around.

THE FINAL NO

I'm not sure where you are in your story.

Maybe you've been trying to get sober for years. Maybe you're still deciding if you even need to. Perhaps you just had the worst drinking night of your life, or maybe you've had so many "worst nights" you lost track a long time ago, along with all your hope. Addiction may be as visible in your life as a hurricane—the wreckage as obvious to you as it is to everyone around you. Or yours may be an internal storm no one knows about, not even the people you live with. You may be acutely addicted or only starting to sense a dependence that makes you uneasy. This may be the first book you've read about sobriety or the thirtieth.

Wherever you are, there's going to be a point you come to where you realize it's up to you. When you're already aware *enough*, knowledgeable *enough*, supported *enough* to do what you need to do to choose sobriety—whatever that means in the moment. We *know* we're at the crossroads when we're there, even if we won't admit it.

Remember the story of bringing Alma to Bertucci's that night for dinner when I almost drank again? I knew.

That time you told yourself you could handle the concert / dinner / happy hour / trip? You knew.

The moment you took the old route home, the one that passes by the liquor store you always popped into, because (you told yourself) it's faster and you're *fine*? You knew.

That day you needed to open your mouth in the support meeting and share, but convinced yourself you didn't have anything important to say, and then the pressure became too much and you had to find some relief? You knew.

That week, month, or stretch of months when you stopped reaching out to other sober people because life got too busy and you were doing great, until you weren't? You knew.

The promise that you'd begin again tomorrow, *again*? You knew.

When you "forgot" to tell your friends, or your parents, or your colleagues, or your date that you weren't drinking before you showed up? You knew.

We know—even if the knowing is a whisper, faint and fleeting.

Sometimes we are simply too physically addicted, too new to sobriety, in too much pain, too traumatized, too buried under the circumstances of our life, without the support or clarity or resources to physically stay sober. This is real.

And sometimes, we don't want to own it. We're not willing to admit that the final no has to come from us.

If you've yet to have that final no—whether that no is to drinking or living in shame in your sobriety, making yourself small to keep the peace, trying to go it alone, or whatever else is keeping you stuck—this part right here is for you. Other people can help you, love you, support you, shock you with their generosity and willingness; the timing can be exactly right and the circumstances aligned, but nothing and no one can make you take responsibility for your life. No one can say the final no but you.

THE BIGGER YES

The final no is only half the story, though. An essential, necessary, and often insanely difficult part—but it's just the first part. It's where a lot of the narratives about addiction stop, unfortunately. We hear about the grueling battle, the years and years of struggle and pain, the ruined relationships and successive bottoms. We hope and pray and wait for that final no, and when it comes—if it comes—we declare victory and celebrate and say, "Wow, what an amazing feat, good for them," and move on.

The person facing sobriety tends to focus on the no, too. What we'll lose if we stop drinking, how our relationships will change, how the color will be drained from our days, and how lonely, boring, and sad it will be to lose this thing we've come to rely on, and even love, so much.

Still, most people can make a list of obvious things that

would improve if they stopped drinking. Big things like less risk of death or jail, fewer health problems, less destruction to our loved ones, less self-hatred, the ability to keep a job. And smaller ones, too: better sleep, paying bills on time, clearer skin, fewer surprising Amazon boxes at our doorstep.

In other words, we can list all the knowns.

But what about the unknowns? What about all the ways your life could change that you've only dared to dream about? What about the things you can't even imagine?

That's what this part is about, and it's the real juice of sobriety for me. That list above is wonderful, excellent, great. But I want you to know that there's more. There's the deeper calling of your soul, the unique potential of your life that only you can fulfill. It's what I call the bigger yes.

What I felt in that room with Liz was this bigger yes calling me forward. I didn't call it that at the time of course, but I can see it clearly in hindsight. Yes, there was the *final no* in that moment, too. But until then, I hadn't felt the full pull of the yes, not like that. I'd experienced flashes of it here and there, like when I'd wake at four A.M. and sit at the kitchen table and write my way into the day, or I'd get positive feedback on a blog post. But I'd never felt it so distinctly as I did that day in the theater, with an author like Liz standing right before me. It was a sliding doors moment—I could feel both what was possible *and* what I stood to lose. It broke my heart and lit it up at the same time.

* *

I'll stop here and ask. *Do you know what I mean?*

Do you have something like this? Something you want to

do, be, or experience so much it aches? A long-held dream you let die, or something that makes no sense because it feels too big, too small, too different, too much like something made for . . . other people?

Maybe it's having children. Or living near the ocean. Traveling to every continent or going to culinary school, opening a restaurant and feeding people beautiful food. Perhaps you have visions of creating spectacular gardens, learning to fish or play the oboe, or becoming a therapist.

Maybe you don't know exactly what it is but you can *feel* it, that big energy pulling at you, telling you there's more to this life. More for you, specifically. I don't mean more money or a better relationship or a renovated kitchen (although there's nothing wrong with wanting those things). I mean the soul-level expression of your life, the potential within you that only you can fulfill.

I didn't have a name for it that day at the event, but I would a few months later when I stumbled upon a book called *The Great Work of Your Life* by Stephen Cope. When I grabbed the book off the shelf and cracked it open, I read the following words:

> If you bring forth what is within you, what you bring forth
> will save you. If you do not bring forth what is within you,
> what you do not bring forth will destroy you.

These words, from the Gospel of Thomas, hit me like a lightning bolt. That was it. The drinking had been killing me, no doubt, but it was knowing I wasn't bringing forth what was within me that was the real death.

Cope's book is about the concept of dharma, a Sanskrit word that appears in the early Vedas and other ancient Hindu texts, and that has several interpretations, including "natural law," "truth," and "the way." I like Stephen Cope's distillation: "The word *dharma* refers to the *peculiar and idiosyncratic qualities of each being*—those essential and particular qualities that make it somehow *itself*."

The idea of pursuing one's purpose as the ultimate meaning of life isn't unique to dharma. Multiple traditions and spiritual teachers, as well as psychologists and philosophers, view "becoming oneself" as the point of our existence. Maslow called it *self-actualization;* Jung called it *individuation;* the Greeks saw it as attaining "gnosis" or an inner knowing that brings one closer to God or the experience of God; in the Bible, it's viewed as something like coming to know and express the Divine within you. Joseph Campbell, who studied multiple theologies as well as mythology, saw it as the unifying point and reward of embarking on what he coined as the Hero's Journey, or the lesser known (but in my view, more profound) Heroine's Journey as depicted by Maureen Murdoch.

In this way, dharma can be seen as our unique blueprint— an essence that exists inside of each person. It's not something we decide for ourselves, but something that's built in, so to speak, like our DNA. It can't be manipulated by our desires (which runs counter to the popular idea that we can be anything we want to be), but instead can only be uncovered and found. Contemplative mystic and scholar Thomas Merton puts it this way: "Every man has a vocation to become someone: but he must understand clearly that in order to fulfill his vocation he can only be one person: himself." (Please substitute *woman* or *person* for *man;* he was not speaking only to men.)

We can only become ourselves.

While this may sound limiting, I find it to be such a massive freaking relief! We can't be anything we want, no, but we *can* become ourselves. In other words, our potential isn't out there somewhere, it's within us—right here, right now. Our job is to uncover it.

To make the idea of dharma more concrete, I like to think about it in terms of animals. Animals aren't confused about the role they play in the animal kingdom. Cats don't try to be dogs or chicken or mice; fish aren't trying to be zebras or birds. Your house cat doesn't get depressed because it can't fly like an eagle or swim like a shark—it just knows (insofar as it *can* know) that it's a cat! It hunts mice, takes naps, bathes itself, and, oddly, probably loves to sit on top of boxes, squeeze into small spaces, and knock shit off your counter. *Why?* Because it's a cat! Yes, each cat has their own individual temperament, personality, and idiosyncratic habits, but at its essence it is a *cat.*

Obviously, humans are a bit more complicated. But also, what if we weren't? What if we could decide not to be? What if so much of our suffering comes from believing we *can* be anyone we want to be—that we can "have it all"—and if we're not chasing that "all," we're failing. What if our ultimate satisfaction and joy were to be found not in trying to be some extraordinary something-or-other kind of person who we're not, but by being the most-us version of who we already are?

The concept of dharma gave me a new way of understanding what I was feeling that day watching Liz. I was seeing something outside of me, yes, but what it awakened in me was a longing for myself. For that bigger yes inside of me. My dharma.

. .

If you're thinking, *Great for you, Laura, but I don't have anything like that*, well—the teachings would say you're wrong. What I've come to understand is that oftentimes, people have a limited view of what a bigger yes should look like—specifically, that it has to relate to profession or how one makes a living, or that it needs to be publicly notable and deemed extraordinary and remarkable by others (thanks, social media). Sometimes, yes, dharma is made visible to others through an achievement, creation, movement, product, service, or otherwise tangible expression, but it's the invisible, inner experience of meaning and purpose that defines it. We all know we can chase and achieve endlessly and still be empty inside.

Let me share some examples:

After getting sober, my friend KC, a musician and self-declared anti-establishment guy, started learning about personal leadership and meditation. Over the course of several years, he studied with Paramahansa Yogananda to develop his meditation practice, became a certified business coach, and eventually left his job in corporate sales to create his own brand of leadership coaching called the Four Permissions. He now coaches some of the top executives and biggest creative forces in the world and wrote what I think of as the first business leadership book with a soul, incorporating elements of music, yoga philosophy, and play into a traditionally dry, type A, results-driven field.

Another friend, Melissa, used her experience overcoming addiction and establishing boundaries to create a free health and wellness movement that has changed the lives of millions of people.

Kelvin, whom you'll meet in the next chapter, drew from his practice of meditation and sound healing when he was incarcerated to become a licensed addiction coach and deliver these healing modalities to other people in recovery.

My friend and colleague Ayanna, after losing her mother to addiction and then overcoming her own, became a social worker and founded a nonprofit called B Free Wellness, which delivers free or low-cost wellness services to people whose lives have been impacted by trauma, addiction, and oppression. She's also an activist for people of color in recovery.

My friend Branden went from living on the streets of Las Vegas to getting his master's degree in psychology and opening one of the country's most successful gyms focused on mind-body health, and later developed the first social-emotional app.

One of the women in my community, Kristi, started her own succulent plant business.

My friend and colleague Tammi Salas finally claimed being an artist and now teaches other people how to tap into their creativity and use art as a healing modality.

Another woman, after getting sober, came into the truth of her sexuality, left her abusive marriage and the dogma of the church she was raised in (that told her being gay was a sin), and came out as a queer.

The list goes on and on; this is a tiny sampling of what I've seen come through people when they've answered the call of their bigger yes. The stories are as varied as our individual lives are, but there is a common thread linking them: Whatever a person's dharma looks like, when they're living in it, they have an unshakable feeling of contentment and a sense of meaning. It's not that their lives are perfect or easy; it's that they're animated by a deep internal knowing—an integrity with who they are and what they're here to do—such that even the suffering in life is colored with purpose.

And while sobriety isn't a requirement for everyone to realize their dharma, I do believe if alcohol is your thing, it's a requirement for you. For whatever reason, it's *your* battle—one of the portals you must walk through—to realize who you are. There's no shortcutting it or hacking your way through, at least as far as I can tell. And again, you don't even have to know what you're running toward, only that there *is* something there, already inside of you. Something that's bigger than the prospect of simply living a life as someone who doesn't drink.

I don't know about you, but for me, this way of thinking changed the game entirely. It's not that it made sobriety easy—it didn't—but it made it *different*. It made it so that I wasn't running away, but toward. It was the energy of love instead of fear, courage instead of despair, faith instead of doubt.

It was the wide-open expansiveness of *yes* instead of the airless constriction of *no*.

It was everything.

QUESTIONS:

What do I need to say a "final no" to?

Am I willing to do it? (Remember: It's only ever a day at a time. How can you commit 100 percent to today?)

How will I say the "final no" today? What specific steps am I going to take?

· ·

I'll end with a story:

There's a classic folktale from Hasidic tradition about a rabbi named Zusya. On his deathbed, Zusya was agitated and upset.

Puzzled, his disciples asked, "Rabbi, why are you sad? You are pious, scholarly, and humble. After all the great things you've done, surely God will judge you favorably."

Zusya said, "Because when I die and have to present myself to the celestial tribune, they will not ask me, 'Zusya, why were you not Moses, or Jeremiah, or Abraham?'"

"They will say, 'Zusya, why were you not Zusya?,' and to this I will have no answer."

Only you can learn the sacred dance of your life. Only you can make the small, quiet choices that move you toward sobriety and into freedom and the fullest expression of you. There will be people all around you to place hands on your back, push you forward, and remind you what's true when you forget. You'll have cheerleaders and teachers and witnesses and guides. But nobody—no single person, no army of support—can love you or care for you enough to bring you all the way home. That job is yours, and only you know if you're fulfilling it.

QUESTIONS:

Is there something specific I long for in the way it's been described in this chapter—as a dharma, my "bigger yes"? What is it? If nothing specific comes to mind, that's okay!

Can I imagine a life where I feel more at ease, more aligned with my values, more joyful and purposeful? Describe in detail what that would look like using the following scenarios.

Note: Don't be afraid to go big. Don't get hung up on what's "reasonable" or "logical" or any other limitations. This is a magic-wand scenario, so let your imagination take hold. Kindly shush any critical, *Who do you think you are?* type of thoughts, and let yourself dream. And, if you're self-conscious about someone else reading those pages later, destroy them when you're done.

A day in the life. Describe a day, from the moment you wake up to the moment you to go sleep, that reflects this kind of existence. What are your surroundings, whom do you interact with, what kinds of conversations

do you have, how do you spend your time at home /
work / in the world, how do you feel and why?

The view from the end. Imagine you've passed on, and
you get to write your own eulogy. What does it include
if you've lived your most fulfilling, integrated, purposeful life? What are your greatest achievements? Of what
are you most proud? Whose lives did you impact posi-
tively, and how? Who attends your funeral and what do
they say? What is your legacy?

8

YOU ARE LOVED.

DURING ONE OF MY WEEKLY MEETINGS FOR THE LUCKIEST CLUB, A man we call "Car Jason," because he always joins our meetings from his car (he gave himself the nickname, not us!), shared that when he joined the community two years ago, he felt confused and even a bit indignant when he first heard number 8, *You are loved.* He said, "I didn't think I could be loved after what my drinking had done to my family. It didn't even occur to me as a possibility. I thought I could get sober, sure, but not that I could be *loved*. Who are these people to say they love me?" He went on to say that over time, through sharing his story, listening to others, practicing honesty, laughing, crying, and everything else that happens in these meetings, he began to feel differently. "Two years later I'm realizing, right now in this meeting, when I hear 'number 8,' I believe it. I don't know, but that feels like a miracle to me."

Oftentimes, when we think of love, we think of a feeling: the way we feel about our partner, our friends, our children, our pets. We'll say we love all kinds of things, every day, from a city to a season to a pair of shoes to the color green. We recognize love as an emotion, a warmth, an affection, a desire. And all these things can be expressions of love, but not the kind of love we're talking about here.

According to the ancient Greeks, there are eight different kinds of love, four of which are well-known: Eros, or erotic, romantic love; Philia, love of friends and equals; Storge, familiar love, like the love parents have for their children; and Agape, which is seen as the highest form of love and the kind of love we're referring to here. Agape is unconditional love that's given without terms or reciprocity. In the Buddhist tradition, it's loving-kindness for all sentient beings as exemplified by the Buddha, and in the Christian tradition, it's believed to be exemplified by the love Jesus exhibited, and the innate essence of God. Agape isn't an emotion, but a choice and a commitment—a deliberate striving toward the highest good. One need not subscribe to any theology or religion to experience or know this kind of love to be real. It can be understood as a universal energy or truth, as scientific as it is spiritual, as present and timeless as stardust. It includes everything and denies nothing. Not even you. And if you don't believe that, you're not the only one. I didn't either. Most of us who fall into the deep darkness don't.

As mysterious as addiction is, so too is the grace of learning love (to give it, to receive it) in recovery. It's not the stuff of Hollywood romance. It's not a quick fix, an instant makeover, bright and shiny, or well-rehearsed. No, this kind of love is gritty, clumsy, and rebellious. It has dirt underneath its fingernails and scars all over its heart. It doesn't always know the right thing to say, but it shows up every damn time, on time. It hangs around after everyone else leaves and finds you wherever you hide. It won't take you on a luxurious trip to Mexico, but it will sit quietly with you in your car for two straight years until you feel it. It won't buy you flowers, but it will hold back your hair when you puke. It will save your life.

How? Through the transformative powers of grace, acceptance, and forgiveness.

LOVE AS GRACE

At thirty-one, Kelvin found himself in jail for the fifth time. This time for domestic assault, which he committed while under the influence of alcohol and drugs.

Kelvin grew up in a strict Baptist home with five siblings. Rules were to be followed and feelings were not discussed. Like most parents, Kelvin's parents did the best they could with the skills and tools they had. At thirteen, Kelvin started to use alcohol and drugs to cope with pain and trauma for the same reason so many of us do: It works. He dropped out of school and made money in whatever ways he could, often by selling drugs. He charged through life, as he says, on autopilot. "I never thought about why I was doing what I was doing or where I was headed—I was in survival mode."

When he landed in jail this time, Kelvin had a three-year-old daughter. He says when he talked to his daughter and her mother on the phone from jail, he could, for the first time, feel how much pain he was causing. Until then, he could never see beyond himself—his own pain, his anger, his needs. Like the drugs and booze, other people were obstacles or ways to fill the ever-present hole inside him. But something about the impact his behavior had on his daughter, and would have on her, created an opening inside him.

He learned he had some resources available to him in prison, which included meditation and sound healing. Sound healing is an ancient meditative practice that uses different musical implements, such as gongs and crystal quartz bowls, to create different frequencies that resonate with different parts of the body and mind. He says when he experienced it for the first time, something inside him shifted. Here he was, in prison, with nearly all his earthly freedoms taken away, and yet he felt a spark of unmistakable freedom inside.

"For the first time, I acknowledged that I had a choice," he says. "I could choose to use drugs in jail as I had before and serve my time, get out, and go back to how I was, or I could decide to use what was being offered, stay sober, and see what happened."

He chose the latter.

Skeptically, he attended every meeting, counseling, and meditation session offered. Countless times he thought, "Men like me, from my family and my neighborhood, don't meditate. Black men in prison don't meditate. We don't do therapy and talk about our feelings." And still he kept going. Slowly, over time, he began to experience an inner shift. "Here, in prison, I felt more free than I ever had on the outside." He said he didn't know what would happen when he got out or if he'd be able to repair his life, find work, or provide for his daughter; he'd dropped out of high school and had a criminal record. But he focused on what was right in front of him, stayed sober, and began to understand the reasons for his past behavior.

Kelvin describes this experience as many things, but one of them is grace. Grace, undeserved favor, an opening where there should be no opening. We can't explain it, we don't deserve it, but still it is there. As Anne Lamott says, "I do not understand the mystery of grace—only that it meets us where we are but does not leave us where it found us."

Every recovery story is laden with grace, including mine. For the sting of every horror we experience, every Godless moment, every assault on our physical body and soul, every offense we commit, we are nonetheless met with moments of grace that manage to pierce through all of it. It arrived as the kind eyes of the EMT who pulled me out of my totaled car despite knowing I had been driving drunk and could have killed someone; a kiss of encouragement on my forehead from my ex-husband when I was first trying to get sober; a poem pressed into my palm from a stranger in a meeting; a break, a breath, a voice, a text, a hand—they come, it comes—and we don't know what, or why, or how . . . and yet.

For Kelvin, it came through sound. For some reason, against all odds, in the cold walls of prison, the vibration of sound broke through and changed him *just* enough in that moment so that he was willing to explore, to see, to try. Grace gave him a portal to walk through, and he did.

Kelvin left prison and stayed sober. Not only that, but he

went back to school, got a degree, and has helped thousands of people in recovery as a recovery coach and counselor. He's got a family, a beautiful relationship with his daughter, and passes on the gifts of meditation and sound healing. Kelvin also leads meetings in The Luckiest Club, which is how I came to know him. One moment of grace after another, and another, and another, and here he is, offering the light of love to the world instead of passing on pain.

QUESTIONS:

Can I identify evidence of love as grace in my life? Moments of undeserved favor?

What did those moments teach me, or what would they teach me, if I allowed the lessons to come through?

LOVE AS ACCEPTANCE

In her second year of her sobriety, my friend Sarah and her wife decided to adopt a rescue dog. It's something they'd talked about doing for years, but as the second winter of the pandemic started to approach and Sarah's depression began to worsen, they felt like it was the right time. Sarah had dogs growing up and yearned for the comfort and emotional support she remembered. She imagined long hikes through the Connecticut woods, snuggles on the couch, and a playmate for their son.

After months of consideration and searching, and then more months of waiting until he gained enough weight to come home, they got Bishop. I am a sucker for dogs as it is, but the first time I saw a picture of Bishop my heart exploded. He was all length and legs, like a newborn deer in a German shepherd / husky / mutt body. Everything about him was long: his nose, his body, his legs, his tail. The expression in his eyes is the one so many dogs have. It says, *Please forgive me; I just want to love you.*

A day or two after they got him, they started to Google symptoms of a lingering cough that he'd had since the shelter took him in. They also noticed he wheezed all the time and didn't have much capacity for exercise. As Sarah said, "He sounded like an eighty-year-old lifetime smoker." They both had the intuitive sense that something was wrong with him, beyond what they already knew from the adoption facility.

They continued to monitor him and carried on. As is normal with a puppy, their routines were turned upside down in those first weeks, but then Sarah got COVID and was laid up for a few weeks. In addition, her depression worsened to a degree she had never experienced before. They both started to feel like maybe it was all too much, but they hoped to find an equilibrium.

When they took Bishop to his first vet visit they learned he had something called laryngeal paralysis, which caused his air passage to be extremely small. It's something that's common in older dogs, but rare in puppies. They were relieved there was an explanation for his wheezing and low tolerance for exercise, and they could now focus on fixing the problem.

"There was this feeling that we just needed to get to a solution, and then he'd be the dog he was supposed to be—the dog we signed up for," said Sarah.

After learning about their options, they decided on a

surgery that would open his airway and had a high rate of success. After the surgery, Sarah and her wife thought they noticed his breathing sounded a little different, but not for long—the wheeze was still there. When her wife left for a trip with their son, Sarah took Bishop for a walk and realized he sounded exactly the same. She took him to the ER, called the surgeon, and it was determined that the surgery hadn't worked. When Sarah brought him back home that night, she went for a walk with him in the woods, and found herself shouting up at the sky, "This is not what I wanted!"

"I'm embarrassed to admit it," she says. "But that's where I was; that's how I felt."

"Our expectations were one thing, and he turned out to be another, and we couldn't figure out why," she said. "We kept asking ourselves, *Is this karma? Is it bad luck? Are we doing something wrong? What is going on here?*"

When Sarah's wife returned from their trip, the two spent the morning talking about what to do. Both of them assumed that the next step was to put Bishop down. They talked about how to break the news to their son. "We were both talking like it had already happened and we just had to get through it."

Then they had a conversation with the surgeon. He said he could perform the surgery again, but that it wasn't likely to be successful. He said they could, of course, put him down, but they could also give him as good of a life as possible, knowing he had this condition and wouldn't live a full life, or a long one. He said, "Listen, you have a sweet, healthy, wonderful dog whose parts don't work. You have a sweet little lemon."

Sarah says during the conversation her internal world started shifting. She realized they weren't going to put him down, and they weren't going to have another surgery either. A different thing was happening.

"I felt terrible that we'd been so sure that we'd put him down, but that's where I was—that's where we were."

After the call with the surgeon, she says her "duty" part showed up first. She went to the kitchen and started looking at what they needed more of: dog food, poop bags, chew toys. "I thought, *Fine. This is our responsibility, and we'll do it.*"

But then she went and sat on the couch with her wife in the living room. Bishop was sitting on the floor next to them resting.

"I don't know why, or what happened, but I suddenly felt like I needed to get down on the floor with him," Sarah recounts. "So I did. I put my face next to his and looked in his face and I said, '*Okay.*'"

She kept saying it, *okay.*

Bishop put his paws on her neck and opened his legs for a belly scratch as she repeated it again and again: *Okay . . . okay . . . okay.*

When I asked her why she said *okay* and what she was saying *okay* to, she said she didn't know why it came out of her, it wasn't conscious, that it came from her body, her heart.

"I was saying *Okay* to him as he was. *Okay* to what was happening instead of what I wanted to happen. *Okay* to him not being what we'd expected. *Okay* to him being the dog that he is. *Okay* to it all."

She says it was the most visceral experience of acceptance she's ever had. "It was a hundred and eighty degrees all at once. Like part of me took a back seat and another part of me stepped forward. And since then, everything with him has been different. I'm open to him, I feel bonded to him."

. .

When Sarah told me this story, knowing her history and what she'd gone through in her two years of sobriety, I smiled, thinking, *Who was accepting who down there on the floor?*

When I asked her if she thinks the experience would have been different if she'd not been sober, she said, "Entirely." She said she wouldn't have been able to tell the truth about how she felt from the beginning because she wouldn't have allowed herself to hear it or feel it, if she even had access to it in the first place. "It would have been too hard to feel that, and I was so disconnected from myself. My drinking was all about not being able to be with what was happening, internally or externally. And so, when it came time, I wouldn't have really accepted anything because I wouldn't have had to burn through my feelings of disappointment, frustration, resentment to arrive there."

This point—the link between acceptance and the truth and, ultimately, love—is so vital, so important. Acceptance doesn't happen without the truth, because *the truth is what one has to accept.* As psychologist Carl Rogers observed, "The curious paradox is that when I accept myself just as I am, then I can change," which could be broadened to say that when we accept *life* as it is—that is, accept the truth—then we can change. If Bishop had been exactly the dog Sarah was hoping for, there would be nothing to accept. If we got exactly the life we hoped for and people behaved exactly like we wanted them to at all times, there would be nothing to accept. If sobriety came easy, there would be nothing to accept. Although we often *think* we'd like life to be this way—easy-peasy, no problems to solve, everything goes our way—we really wouldn't. A life without challenge is not only boring; it's meaningless.

· ·

That moment on the floor with Bishop and Sarah exemplifies the gift of acceptance. It's not as though anything actually changed in that moment—Bishop wasn't magically healed and Sarah's heart was still broken—but she was able to hold these things differently: with grace, and a lightness that wasn't there before. When we find acceptance, our problems are still there; they just sting less. We are still who we are, with all our mistakes and pain, but we can somehow bear those mistakes and pain more easily.

Acceptance itself *is* the single-word incantation of *okay*. Repeated again, and again, and again, we slowly fall into the decision and the allowance, the stepping forward and the letting go, the catch and the release, until we are at rest, at ease, at home.

QUESTIONS:

Can you identify evidence of love as acceptance in your life? Are there people (or animals, or parts of nature, or an expression of God) that accept you exactly as you are, even if and when you cannot?

To what, or to whom, do you need to say "okay" in your life, the way Sarah did?

How would being able to say "okay" change your life, or the lives of those around you?

LOVE AS FORGIVENESS

Mike had been sober for several years when he made a direct amends to his ex-wife, the mother of his two kids. A couple of months later, she invited him to come over for Thanksgiving with their kids and extended family. While she was serving pumpkin soup to everyone, Mike recognized the bowls she was using and said, "Oh, I remember this pottery!"

He noticed her expression shifted a bit as she replied, "Oh . . . yeah."

"Was there a story there?" he asked.

"Yeah," she replied, clearly wanting to move on.

"No, tell me! Come on, I'm trying not to forget the past or shut the door on it," he said, using the language from AA.

"Okay . . . you remember when you won that golf tournament that year?"

"Yeah."

"Remember you were drunk for a week after?"

"Yeah."

"And the day of the tournament you ran up the big bar bill?"

"Yeah."

"Well," she said, "We couldn't pay the bill off, and so I went to work selling Tupperware, and out of that work I got a coupon for merchandise and I used it to buy this pottery."

"Ahhh, shit," Mike said, hanging his head. He started to choke up a little when she said, "*Hey!*" finding his eyes so they could meet hers.

"Listen," she said. "That was then. This is now. I understand you don't drink anymore. And I certainly don't pay off other people's bar bills anymore. We've got two fine children, these wonderful grandchildren, and some fond memories together. And I have some beautiful pottery."

She stood up to walk back into the kitchen, and on her way there, passed by Mike, touched his cheek softly, leaned in close, and whispered, "Just let it go."

. .

When Mike told me this story, he'd just passed thirty-five years of sobriety. When I asked him if he was able to let it go after that, he said, "Well, I realized it was my choice then. She'd already forgiven me, so the question was whether I would."

I knew exactly the place he was at. I had been there myself. In many cases—with my ex-husband, family members, ex-colleagues, friends—it was clear to me, when I talked to them and made my own amends in sobriety, or resurfaced old events that weighed on me, that I'd been hanging on to my mistakes from drinking much more tightly than they had. But there were and are many, many cases—for me, for Mike, and others—where people won't forgive us, no matter what we do or how much time passes. And so, in both scenarios, we are left with the same choice: *Will we forgive ourselves?*

The word *forgiveness* stems from the Germanic translation of Vulgar Latin, *perdonare,* which means "to give up desire or power to punish."

To give up desire or power to punish.

While our instincts and our conditioning all point us toward punishment as the way to motivate ourselves into change, the professional, personal, and spiritual research on this is clear: It doesn't work. As Dr. Kristin Neff, professor, author, and pioneering researcher on self-compassion, says, "If you really want to motivate yourself, love is more powerful than fear." In other words, are we willing to give up the *desire and power to punish ourselves*?

Your honest answer right now may be no. I've been there. I used to think *Who am I to let myself off the hook? How could I when I've caused so much harm?* It didn't even feel like a choice I could make, but here's the truth: It is. If you sit with the question a little longer, you'll find it is a choice. And here's how I know. When I asked myself if I would punish Alma in the way I punished myself, even if she'd done everything I'd done and more, the answer was so clear: *Never. No. I wouldn't even think of it. I couldn't.* When I asked myself if I would forgive her, the answer was *Yes. Easily. Obviously. Without question.* You don't have to be a parent to ask yourself this; consider anything or anyone that you love naturally, easily, without condition.

So why, then? Why would I not offer myself the same forgiveness? The answer has to do with so many of the things we've already talked about: shame, blame, culture, society. But the part we haven't talked about, which is the best argument for forgiving oneself in my opinion, is that *we have to be what we want to pass on*. No matter how much love, kindness, forgiveness, grace, acceptance, and compassion we shower on others, as long as we can't offer that to ourselves as well, it may as well be for naught. I've mentioned several times that pain and dysfunction are passed down from generation to generation. To truly stop this cycle, we have to establish new modes of operating; we have to, as Kristin Neff says, "step out of the system." We have to give up the desire and power to punish other people, yes, but also ourselves. We have to stop punishing ourselves.

This realization came to me while on a train to work sometime in my second year of sobriety, after an awful morning with Alma. I'd woken up late, she'd put up a fight getting dressed, and as the minutes ticked by my patience wore out. In what felt like the hundredth attempt to get her to put on her pants I snapped, smacked her on the butt, and started screaming at the top of my lungs. Naturally, she burst into tears. Then I started crying, too, and by the time I dropped her off at school—where I'd be leaving her all day, until I picked her up at six o'clock that night—I was wrung out, empty. I felt like I had no business being a mother. Even sober, I acted like a feral animal. I felt wretched, no different from when I had been drinking.

In moments like this, all the old shame surfaced, like it had been waiting for me. All the horrors of my drinking flashed through my mind. I'd picture the image of her little body walking alone and scared through the halls of the hotel at my brother's wedding, looking for me; driving drunk with her countless times; drinking too much at her birthday parties; reading to her half-buzzed at bedtime, being impatient when I was hungover (I was always hungover). It still felt so near that I could smell the wine on my skin, feel the long string of insults to her innocence. It was like being slapped again, and again, and again.

When I got on the train, I sat near the window and pushed my forehead against the cool glass, willing myself to calm down so I could function at work. I had a big client meeting first thing, which was part of the reason I was so anxious about being late. After a while, as we rolled closer to Boston, I checked Instagram and saw I'd received a direct message from a sober guy I'd been following who lived in Coney Island. We'd never talked directly before, only commented on each other's posts from time to time. I knew he had a ton of years sober, something like twenty. In his message, he sent me an image of a poem that ended with these words.

come with your swollen heart
i've never seen anything more beautiful than you.

His message: Thought you might need this. Keep your head up, kiddo.

The poem, by Warsan Shire, is titled "first thought after seeing you smile." In it, she speaks about coming with every secret and lie that haunts you, every regret that keeps you up at night, and every failure, every bitter, shameful thing. She mentions drinks, blackouts, and sins. In this short piercing poem, she named every unspeakable part of me in such a visceral way, it was as if she'd plunged her fist into my chest. She named all the mistakes that I believed would forever supplant any goodness inside me, no matter how hard I tried, or how sorry I was, or how long I stayed sober. But then those lines, that last line: *I've never seen anything more beautiful than you.*

I'd never heard of Warsan Shire, had never seen these words before, and didn't know the man who sent them. But somehow, they'd found me. Somehow they'd reached right into my heart and changed it.

I cried and I cried and I cried, but the tears were different from the ones that came earlier. They were the tears of relief and release, not anger and defeat. I suppose I could have taken many things from her words, but what I kept hearing over and over was this: *Sweet girl, you are already forgiven*. It came through in a voice that was mine but not me—as clear as a cloudless sky. *Sweet girl, you are already forgiven*.

When Mike told me the story of his ex-wife, I immediately thought of that morning on the train. Although the circumstances and the messengers were different, the message was the same: We were already forgiven; it was now ourselves we had to set free.

As long as I continued to pin every difficult moment of parenting to the shame of my drinking, I would keep us— both me and Alma—imprisoned there. By making what I'd done in my addiction the measuring stick of my worth as a mother and allowing those mistakes to define me, I would show her that her mistakes are what ultimately defined her, too. I would teach her that perfection was the only way to be worthy of love, and eventually—as I had, as so many of us have—she would learn to live on the awful treadmill that never stopped, chasing the thing that could never be had. It wasn't noble to hold myself to the cross, it was ruinous—and not only to me, which I could have probably lived with, but to her, which I could not. By keeping my mistakes close and never truly allowing myself to move past them, I would keep them alive forever. It wasn't honorable; it was foolish. Not drinking was a significant step forward, but the destruction would still continue, even in sobriety, as long as I waged these silent wars on myself. I'd lived with generations of people who waged those wars; I'm sure you have, too. If I was going to step out and break this cycle, I had to actually step out. Get off the treadmill. Choose me. Choose her. Choose love. It felt radical because it was.

That moment didn't change everything for me all at once, of course. I still had to wade through all kinds of old memories and feelings to arrive at a place of forgiveness, and I still bump up against my old patterns from time to time. But like those initial moments of grace and acceptance I've laid out, this moment created an opening for me to walk through, and I did. So did Mike at Thanksgiving dinner with his wife. So did Car Jason, sitting in his driveway, each time he tuned in to a meeting.

. .

One of the most touching moments I've ever witnessed was during an interview Oprah did in the late eighties with a mother who had watched her son die. The mother recounts crawling into his bed with him right before he passed. His last words to her were "Oh, it was all so simple." And then he smiled and passed on.

Oh, it was all so simple.

Although the meaning behind his words wasn't explained, it didn't need to be. To explain it would have been futile, cheap, frustrating—like trying to explain love—because that's exactly what he was talking about. In the end, beneath our dramas and fights and stories and everything we get turned around by and spun out on, all we are here to do, to be, to learn, is love. *It's so simple.*

In the beginning, it is simple. In the end, it is simple again. In between, in the process of living, things get complicated and we get confused. But what if that's the whole design? What if the ways we get lost aren't the problem at all? When you think about it, how could it be any other way? If we didn't know the pain of being lost, how would we appreciate the miracle of coming home?

The turn from addiction to recovery always starts with a single moment of grace, acceptance, or forgiveness. We bring our most broken selves to something or someone else, expecting to be turned away, shunned, ridiculed—*surely, they haven't seen the likes of me before,* we think—and we are instead let in. Where we expect a reaction, there is none; there is only a quiet nod of knowing. We don't understand it and we don't need to. As Paul Tillich said, "You are accepted. You are accepted, accepted by that which is greater than you, and the name of which you do not know. Do not ask for the name now; perhaps you will find it later. Do not try to do anything now; perhaps later you will do much. Do not seek for anything; do not perform anything; do not intend anything. Simply accept the fact that you are accepted."

Simply accept the fact that you are accepted. Held in grace. Forgiven already. Then one day—perhaps soon, perhaps in many years—you will find yourself doing something entirely ordinary: stirring cream into your coffee, digging around for a match to a sock, turning your key into the door, stepping off an airplane, kissing your child good night, petting the velvety ear of your cat, sitting in your car for the thousandth time listening to a once-stranger on the internet talk about love. And you will be struck with the sudden realization that what had once sounded foreign and impossible is now yours: that love lives inside you, that it always has.

You'll say, *Oh, it was all so simple.*
Okay.

QUESTIONS:

If forgiveness is giving up the power or desire to punish others, whom do you need to forgive?

What would forgiveness look like here?

Are you willing to take those steps? Why, or why not?

What would make you willing?

If self-forgiveness is giving up the power or desire to punish yourself, what do you need to forgive yourself for?

What would forgiveness look like here?

Are you willing to take those steps? Why, or why not?

What would make you willing?

9

WE WILL NEVER STOP REMINDING YOU OF THESE THINGS.

IN THE SUMMER OF 2020, SEVERAL MONTHS INTO THE PANDEMIC and lockdowns, I found myself standing on the shore of the ocean holding a bottle of pills. They were sleeping pills, Ambien, prescribed by my doctor because about a month prior I'd told her—like God knows how many other people—that I couldn't sleep and my anxiety had spiked. I was waking up in the middle of the night in a cold sweat, mind racing, afraid of nothing I could name but also everything. Anxiety has been both my Achilles' heel and a blessing. When I finally stopped drinking it was, more than anything else, the visceral memory of anxiety that kept me from drinking in the moments when I wanted to. All I'd have to do when the urge came on was close my eyes and imagine feeling that ice in my veins, the nearness of death, the haunting, endless, horrific thoughts, and I'd shake my head, *No. No no no no.* I couldn't. I wouldn't survive it.

But taking sleeping medication was a slippery slope, and I knew it. It had taken some real honesty and effort for me to give up Ambien three years earlier. I'd taken it more or less steadily for ten years, aside from my pregnancy. What started out as a sleep aid became a way to check out (although I swore it was about the sleep, and I had become dependent on it because it is physically addictive). As the years ticked on in sobriety, I realized my attachment to it too closely mirrored my attachment to alcohol: It took up far too much brain space and I was secretive about using it (always a tip-off). So, I stopped taking it and learned to fall asleep, or not—and stay asleep, or not—without medication.

Then March 2020 hit. I had been on tour for *We Are the Luckiest* since January, traveling across the United States, meeting and talking to people and realizing this lifelong dream of publishing a book, when everything suddenly stopped. Like the rest of us, I canceled plans and started to live in twenty-four-hour increments, sometimes one-hour increments. My response in crisis has always been to over-function. I've joked that I'm great in an emergency and it's true: I know exactly what to do and you totally want me by your side, but the downside is, when I'm operating in that space, I get cut off from my heart. For short periods of time, this is fine, but not for months (and what would be years) on end; not with no end in sight.

Getting cut off from our hearts is dangerous. All that life force has to go somewhere, and if it can't flow freely between ourselves and others, it eventually transmutes into something dark and destructive. We all saw this in the pandemic. In the absence of being able to connect and feel, I became anxious.

In fact, I became so anxious so quickly that I became terrified. So I fell back on my default coping mechanism, and I looked for an escape hatch: I called my doctor and told her I needed help, knowing full well she'd prescribe me something to sleep. I felt justified in doing it and ignored that little voice inside me saying: *careful.*

I took the medicine before bed for a few days and, like it had done before, it knocked me out for the night but made my anxiety spike the next day. I considered taking pills during the day so I could fall asleep for a few hours and catch my breath. A couple of times I did, and told no one.

Then, in an unlikely turn of events given the circumstances, I met someone. I *really* liked him and there's nothing on the entire planet more anxiety-inducing for me than the terrain of new love. I know for most people it's this wonderful, exciting, glorious time. But for me? Torture.

I'd also started The Luckiest Club and was trying to navigate the bizarre, awful world of co-parenting during a pandemic where each transfer of homes was a potential death risk. Friends and family were getting sick; some had died. I was, like everyone else, doing my best to put out my own individual fires while watching the world at large go up in flames.

But the pills. I woke one morning in my new love's bed, shaky, my veins filled with the anxiety ice from having taken one of them before bed, and I knew what I had to do. Despite my fear of not sleeping, of the anxiety, of feeling everything that was slamming against my heart, I knew there was no real escape in escape. I knew there was only one way through.

So I walked downstairs, down the slope of the backyard, and onto the shore, took off my shoes, and waded into the

water. I opened the bottle and threw the pills into the outgo-
ing tide, a spray of tiny peach flecks, and watched them float
away. They looked so innocent, so tiny for the power they had
over me, and what I knew they could lead to. I whispered, *Go.*
I bent over to put my hands on my knees, and cried. Finally.

Then I did the next right thing, which was to call someone
and tell them. No more secrets.

. .

That experience was, above all, humbling. I thought—as I
have countless times in sobriety—I should be further along,
better, *past that.* Even though I say things EVERY SINGLE
DAY like *Life never stops being life. This is a process. We never fully
arrive.* I still couldn't remember it in the moment. I still forgot.
In the midst of the unknown, I had fallen back on my oldest,
tried-and-true coping mechanisms: over-functioning, going it
alone, and staying quiet because *that's what I do.* It's what we all
do. Not "people like us," everyone, all humans. In the absence
of regular practice and community, we forget and fall back on
what we know.

Every so often in a recovery meeting or elsewhere, someone will say something like *I don't want this to be my life. I don't
want to have to work so hard all the time. I don't want to talk about
drinking or not drinking forever. I want to move on.* And I get it—
I completely get it. I've gone through periods of "recovery
burnout" many times. Usually, it's because I've been pushing
too hard and treating myself like an endless self-improvement
project. But what I've come to understand is that anything we
value and want to keep alive and healthy and vibrant, needs

attention and tending. Relationships. Our bodies. Homes. Plants. It's the way of things.

At first, sobriety takes everything. It's all-consuming. But as time goes on—if we do give it all our effort and attention—that changes. I've said the progression goes something like this: impossible, difficult, strange, normal, wouldn't have it any other way. The progression is made possible by consistent effort over time.

This is why number 9 is a promise: to remind, to remember, and to do it together. Because as long as we never stop reminding one another of these things, we stay the course. We avoid the place where, as Jeff Tweedy sang, our "blessings get so blurred," and we forget what it is we're fighting for.

But also: If we do forget, it's okay. We just come back. The invitation remains open. The nine things are a door that never closes, a promise that never ends.

In The Luckiest Club, we've developed a shorthand speak in meetings, online, or when we see each other in real life: number 8 (You are loved). If someone is sharing something painful in a meeting, the chat box lights up with a string of number 8s. When someone comes back to another Day 1: number 8. When someone hits a year, or two, or ten: number 8. It's the essential message, the promise, the prayer, the thing beneath all the other things.

You are loved.

· ·

When I think about recovery, I imagine structures that are both flexible and strong, like oak trees with their extensive, invisible root systems that allow the visible part of the tree to bear its ever-changing environment, and skyscrapers with their meticulously planned architecture, which provide enough space for the building to move without toppling or collapsing when the earth shakes, while also being solid enough to hold its hundred-thousand-ton structure.

Each day that I practice sobriety—which is, as I see it now, being as present and as honest as possible—I am a little bit stronger. A bit more fortified in my ability to face anything and not look away. And so I'm able to contribute more healing to the world than destruction, even if some days that takes place only in the confines of my own mind. That's what this is all for, in the end, you know? A little less destruction each day. A little more light.

In this way, bit by bit, we become like the oak tree, the skyscraper. Roots deep, heart stretched toward the sky, flexible and strong enough to change the world.

CONCLUSION

ON A FOGGY JUNE DAY IN THE SUMMER OF 2014, I STOOD AT LANDS
End Lookout in San Francisco overlooking the Pacific Ocean.
I grabbed my phone to take a photo and saw that a friend
had just sent me a text. In it was a link to an essay by John
O'Donohue.

As my hair whipped across my face and the ocean spray
cast tiny droplets onto the phone screen, I began to read it.

If you could imagine the most incredible story ever, it
would be less incredible than the story of being here.

My heart swelled into my throat. I knew I was standing
at the threshold of the most incredible story ever. And it was
mine. Although I had not yet had my last drink, I knew it was
coming—that it *could* come—if I kept reaching for the light.

And it did, of course. I did. With the help of one thousand angels, I kept reaching day after day for the past eight years. In that time, I've witnessed thousands of others do the same.

· ·

My friend and mentor Dani Shapiro once told me a story about her beloved aunt Shirley. Shirley had instructed Dani at several points in her life, when she was faced with a situation where she might choose, even justifiably, to allow the status quo to carry forward—where resentment, dysfunction, or indifference would be easier, and easy to understand—to instead go first. To be the one to do it differently. To take the step into the unknown because—well, because, why not her? Who else, if not her? "You be the one," she'd say. "You go and be the one."

These words kept surfacing so often over the past year I finally wrote them down on a piece of paper that sits on my desk, and then I started saying them to myself out loud as I was chipping away at the book, at life, at this elusive "new normal" we were all seeking post-pandemic. I didn't really even understand how it applied in many moments, but it wouldn't leave me alone.

As I approached the end of writing this book and considered what I wanted to leave you with, it was clear. It was this.

You be the one.

You be the one to forgive, even when they don't deserve it.

You be the one to let go, even when it leaves them behind.

You be the one to write that permission slip—the one you've been waiting for all your life.

You be the one to cast the new mold, take the first step, shape the world as it needs to be.

You be the one who says *yes* when the answer has always been *no*.

You be the hope.

You be the brave.

You be the house where the truth is told.

You be the one who says, *Help*, and you be the one to give it.

You be the one who chooses you.

You be the one who chooses your life, the most incredible story ever, the story of being here.

You be the one to push off from here.

ACKNOWLEDGMENTS

I'D HEARD THAT WRITING A SOPHOMORE BOOK IS ESPECIALLY challenging, and naturally, I didn't get why until I was in it. I can attest that "especially challenging" is accurate—to the degree that, at many points, I nearly (seriously) gave up while writing this book. Somehow, I didn't, and that's only because I had a village of people behind me. My name is the only one on the cover, but without that village, this book wouldn't exist.

First, to the team at Ballantine, and especially to my editor, Sara Weiss, as well as Kara Welsh, who decided they believed in me, my work, and this book, and took a shot. Sara, you've been a dream to work with and I'm so grateful to have you on my team. Also, to Sydney Collins, Quinne Rogers, Kathleen Quinlan, Emily Isayeff, Susan Turner, and the rest of the team at Random House.

To my agent Jamie Carr (and the whole team at The Book

Group!), you're just the best! I will never forget that phone call or the hysterical laughter. Here's to many, many, many more of those.

To Heidi Feinstein, my fairy godmother, I am endlessly grateful for you and I will always, always pay it forward.

To KC, for your wizardry and megawatt light, you've helped me, challenged me, annoyed me (lol), consoled me, patiently listened to me, and kept me focused. Everyone should be so stupidly lucky to have someone like you in their corner.

To Elissa Altman, who read the earliest drafts of these pages and provided expert editorial guidance and endless emotional encouragement when I needed it most.

To Brooke Mays, who will always be the OG lady wizard, thank you, for everything.

To Emily Paulson, Christie Tate, Anne Lamott, Elena Brower, and Kelly McDaniel, who were the first readers, for your kindness and generosity and assurances—all of which brought my anxiety down to a somewhat manageable level.

To Mikel Ellcessor, the other half of *Tell Me Something True* podcast, for being such an incredible creative collaborator and friend.

To the whole TLC team, where do I even begin? You all kept me alive, quite literally, during the height of the pandemic. For the humor and the humility and the fun and the sorrow and the work and the play and all of it—it's all been a total God shot.

To my Boston girls, especially Kate, I love you forevs.

To my MHD crew, you are my home.

To my mom and Derek and my brother and Jenny and

Shane and Gavin. Thank you for supporting me always, and I'm sorry you have to be related to a writer.

To Taylor Swift, who is a complete genius creator, who never stops inspiring me, whom I will shamelessly fangirl until I die, and who also got me through the pandemic with the art that are the *folklore* and *evermore* albums. This is me trying.

To Robin Arzón, Cody Rigsby, Tunde Oyeneyin, and Christine D'Ercole, who unknowingly became my best friends during the pandemic and kept me from quitting on this book.

To every single person who has supported and encouraged me since I started writing and talking about addiction and sobriety in 2013. To the original HOME listeners, the social media folks, the blog readers and the podcast listeners. Growing up in public has been weird at the very least, but you've let me do it, and do it awkwardly most of the time, and sometimes very poorly. As awful as the internet can be, it can be pretty fucking magical too. Thanks for the magic.

To Todd, who showed up right on time, but also, what took so long? You said early on, "Let's go big, you and me," and I just keep saying yes. Thank you for showing me what it means to be loved well; you are a miracle and a dream.

To Alma, for whom there will never be enough words, or time, or love (though I'll always try!). You'll never have to earn your place in my heart; it belongs to you.

And lastly, to every noodle who ever has been or ever will be, I hope this book meets you exactly where you need to be met. I will never stop reminding you of these things.

NOTES

INTRODUCTION

xii **"It is not your fault":** Laura McKowen, *We Are the Luckiest: The Surprising Magic of a Sober Life* (Novato, Calif.: New World Library, 2020), epigraph.

xx **Prior to the 1930s, alcoholism:** Griffith Edwards, *Alcohol: The World's Favorite Drug* (New York: Thomas Dunne, 2002), 103–17.

xx **be committed to a long-term treatment in an asylum:** Susan Cheever, "Time 100: Bill Wilson," *Time*, March 31, 2007, 201.

xxi **there are more than two million AA members:** "Estimated Worldwide A.A. Individual and Group Membership," last modified December 2021, accessed August 14, 2022, https://www.aa.org/estimated-worldwide-aa-individual-and-group-membership.

xxi **around two-thirds of addiction treatment facilities:** Substance Abuse and Mental Health Services Administration, *National Survey of Substance Abuse Treatment Services (N-SSATS): 2020* (Rockville, Md.: Substance Abuse and Mental Health Services Administration, 2021).

xxii **"Try not to condemn your alcoholic husband":** *Alcoholics Anonymous Big Book*, 4th ed. (New York: Alcoholics Anonymous World Services, 2002), 104.

xxiii **narratives that were often developed and paid for:** Peter

Miller, "How Big Alcohol Is Trying to Fool Us into Thinking Drinking Is Safer Than It Really Is," *The Conversation*, October 21, 2019, https://theconversation.com/how-big-alcohol-is-trying-to-fool-us -into-thinking-drinking-is-safer-than-it-really-is-125309.

xxv **There's a large, growing body of research about:** "Psychedelics Research and Psilocybin Therapy," last modified October 18, 2021, accessed August 14, 2022, https://www.hopkinsmedicine.org/ psychiatry/research/psychedelics-research.html.

xxvi **Seane Corn, who says trauma is defined as:** "Yoga, Trauma, and Tension—A Conversation with Seane Corn," *Wanderlust*, accessed November 12, 2021, https://wanderlust.com/journal/yoga -trauma-and-tension-a-conversation-with-seane-corn/.

xxvii **"the world is experienced with a different nervous system":** Bessel van der Kolk, *The Body Keeps the Score: Brain, Mind, and Body in the Healing of Trauma* (New York: Penguin, 2014), 82.

xxvii **trauma exists on a continuum that's impacted by:** Amanda E. White, *Not Drinking Tonight: A Guide to Creating a Sober Life You Love* (New York: Hachette, 2022), 34.

xxviii **"The normal way never leads home":** John O'Donohue, "The Question Holds The Lantern," *The Sun*, November, 2009, https:// thesunmagazine.org/issues/407/the-question-holds-the-lantern.

xxviii **"building a life [you] don't want, or need, to escape from":** Holly Whitaker, *Quit Like a Woman* (New York: Dial Press, 2019), 190.

1 IT IS NOT YOUR FAULT.

8 **"Believing you are good is like believing":** Thomas Lloyd Qualls, *Waking Up at Rembrandt's* (Reno, Nev.: Lucky Bat Books, 2013).

15 **ACE Study, a 1998:** Vincent Felitti et al., "Relationship of Childhood Abuse and Household Dysfunction to Many of the Leading Causes of Death in Adults: The Adverse Childhood Experiences (ACE) Study," *American Journal of Preventive Medicine* 14, no. 4 (May 1998): 245–58, https://doi.org/10.1016/S0749-3797(98)00017-8.

15 **individuals who have an ACE score of 4:** "The Role of Adverse Childhood Experiences in Substance Misuse and Related Behavioral Health Problems," SAMHSA'S Center for the Application of Prevention Technologies, accessed August 14, 2022, https://pubmed .ncbi.nlm.nih.gov/31104722/.

16 **"Addiction shouldn't be called 'addiction'":** Jane Ellen Stevens, "Addiction Doc Says: It's Not the Drugs. It's the ACEs . . . Adverse Childhood Experiences," *Aces Too High News*, May 2, 2017,

https://acestoohigh.com/2017/05/02/addiction-doc-says-stop
-chasing-the-drug-focus-on-aces-people-can-recover/.

17 **In the movie *Good Will Hunting*:** *Good Will Hunting*, directed by
Gus Van Sant, Miramax, 1997.

18 **The tendency for trauma victims to blame themselves:**
Tanya Clausen, LCSW, "Self-Blame," Ross Center, December 16,
2019, https://www.rosscenter.com/news/self-blame/.

18 **"What human beings cannot contain of their experience":**
M. Gerard Fromm, *Lost in Transmission: Studies of Trauma Across Generations* (Oxfordshire, UK: Routledge, 2019).

20 ***Alcohol is both the deadliest drug*:** Kelly Fitzgerald, "Why Alcohol Is the Deadliest Drug," Addiction Center, updated October 12,
2021, https://www.addictioncenter.com/community/why-alcohol
-is-the-deadliest-drug/.

20 **And yet, alcohol is the *most harmful drug*:** David J. Nutt,
Leslie A. King, and Lawrence D. Phillips, "Drug Harms in the UK:
A Multicriteria Decision Analysis," *The Lancet*, November 10, 2010,
https://www.thelancet.com/journals/lancet/article/PIIS0140
-6736(10)61462-6/.

20 **in the United States, alcohol is now the third leading cause:**
"Alcohol Facts and Statistics," National Institute on Alcohol Abuse
and Alcoholism, updated March 2022, https://www.thelancet.com/
journals/lancet/article/PIIS0140-6736(10)61462-6/.

21 **Global spending on alcohol advertising is expected:** "Big
Alcohol Exposed: Big Investments in Advertising Onslaught,"
Movendi International, May 28, 2021, https://movendi.ngo/
news/2021/05/28/big-alcohol-exposed-big-investments-in
-advertising-onslaught/.

21 **alcohol beverage sales in 2020:** Jan Conway, "Market Share of
the U.S. Alcohol Industry by Beverage 2000–2021," Statista, February 20, 2022, https://www.statista.com/statistics/233699/market
-share-revenue-of-the-us-alcohol-industry-by-beverage/.

22 **the 2018 report in *The Lancet*:** Max G. Griswold et al., "Alcohol
Use and Burden for 195 Countries and Territories, 1990–2016: A
Systematic Analysis for the Global Burden of Disease Study 2016,"
The Lancet 392, no. 10152 (August 23, 2018): https://doi
.org/10.1016/S0140-6736(18)31310-2.

22 **"Based on recent evidence":** "The Impact of Alcohol Consumption on Cardiovascular Health: Myths and Measures: A World Heart
Federation Policy Brief," World Heart Federation, February 2022,
https://world-heart-federation.org/wp-content/uploads/WHF
-Policy-Brief-Alcohol.pdf.

23 **"The alcohol industry has also perpetuated":** Ibid.

24 **qualify as alcoholic in AA's quiz:** "Twelve Questions Only You Can Answer," Alcoholics Anonymous, accessed October 3, 2021, https://www.aa.org/self-assessment.

24 *as in a fourteen-million-people-wide spectrum:* "Understanding Alcohol Use Disorder," National Institute on Alcohol Abuse and Alcoholism, last modified April 2021, https://www.niaaa.nih.gov/publications/brochures-and-fact-sheets/understanding-alcohol-use-disorder.

25 **only about 5 percent will get treatment:** Rachel N. Lipari and Struther L. Van Horn, "Trends in Substance Use Disorders Among Adults Age 18 or Older," Substance Abuse and Mental Health Services Administration, June 29, 2017, https://www.samhsa.gov/data/sites/default/files/report_2790/ShortReport-2790.html.

25 **For women in the United States:** Jennifer Clopton, medically reviewed by Neha Pathak, "Alcohol Consumption Among Women Is on the Rise," *WebMD*, July 18, 2018, https://www.webmd.com/women/news/20180718/alcohol-consumption-among-women-is-on-the-rise.

25 **Alcohol use kills nearly four thousand U.S. teens each year:** "Alcohol and Public Health," Centers for Disease Control and Prevention, updated April 14, 2022, https://www.cdc.gov/alcohol/fact-sheets/underage-drinking.htm.

28 **"Brain-imaging studies":** "Biology of Addiction: Drugs and Alcohol Can Hijack Your Brain," National Institutes of Health, https://newsinhealth.nih.gov/2015/10/biology-addiction.

28 **"A common misperception is that addiction":** Ibid.

28 **"allergy to alcohol":** *Alcoholics Anonymous Big Book*, xxiv.

28 **"We know that while the alcoholic keeps away":** Ibid., 22.

30 **It's a defense mechanism that arises when we cannot reconcile:** Neel Burton, "Self-Deception II: Splitting," *Psychology Today*, updated May 4, 2020, https://www.psychologytoday.com/us/blog/hide-and-seek/201203/self-deception-ii-splitting.

2 IT IS YOUR RESPONSIBILITY.

35 **"Until we bring what is unconscious into consciousness":** The original source of this quotation is unknown, but it is commonly attributed to Carl Jung.

52 **How am I choosing, creating, or attracting this situation?:** Christopher Avery, *The Responsibility Process: Unlocking Your Natural Ability to Live and Lead with Power* (Pflugerville, Tex.: Partnerwerks, 2016), 198.

53 **"Many traumatized people expose themselves":** Bessel van der Kolk, "The Compulsion to Repeat the Trauma," *Psychiatric Clinic of North America*, 12, no. 2 (June 1989), 389–411.

54 **In her seminal book** *Mindset,* **Dr. Carol Dweck discovered:** Carol S. Dweck, *Mindset: The New Psychology of Success* (New York: Ballantine, 2016).

59 **We tend to catastrophize how bad we will feel:** Daniel Todd Gilbert, *Stumbling on Happiness* (London: Harper, 2007).

60 **during World War I, it was not uncommon:** Steven Pressfield, *Turning Pro: Tap Your Inner Power and Create Your Life's Work* (New York: Black Irish Entertainment, 2012), 50.

60 **"The habits and addictions of the amateur":** Ibid., 50.

61 **"below the line of responsibility":** Avery, *Responsibility Process,* 61.

3 IT'S UNFAIR THAT THIS IS YOUR THING.

65 **slow, elusive becoming of addiction:** Caroline Knapp, *Drinking: A Love Story* (New York: Dial Press, 1996), 7.

66 **"This sucks!":** Ibid., 270.

68 **"Shame needs three things to grow":** Brené Brown, *The Gifts of Imperfection*, 10th ed. (Center City, Minn.: Hazelden Publishing, 2020), 53.

70 **"I know. It** *does* **suck":** Knapp, *Drinking*, 271.

70 **emotional validation is among:** Kristalyn Salters-Pedneault, "What Is Emotional Validation?," *Very Well Mind*, March 24, 2020, https://www.verywellmind.com/what-is-emotional-validation -425336.

70 **"The moment we believe":** Tara Brach, *Radical Acceptance* (New York: Bantam Dell, 2004), 107.

75 **joy—the most vulnerable:** Brené Brown, *Daring Greatly* (New York: Gotham, 2012), 117.

4 THIS IS YOUR THING.

77 **"Pain travels through families":** The original source of this quote is unknown, but it is commonly attributed to Stephanie Wagner.

80 **Alcoholics Anonymous quiz:** "Twelve Questions Only You Can Answer," Alcoholics Anonymous, accessed October 3, 2021, https://www.aa.org/self-assessment. There are numerous variations on this quiz.

87 **"It's hard to get enough":** The original source of this quote is unknown, but it is commonly attributed to Vincent Felitti, MD.

91 **our inability to accurately predict:** Shahram Heshmat, "6 Mental Traps in Predicting Future Feelings," *Psychology Today*, June 18, 2018, https://www.psychologytoday.com/us/blog/ science-choice/201806/6-mental-traps-in-predicting-future -feelings.

91 **"I forget about you":** Taylor Swift, "All Too Well," track 5 on *Red*, Big Machine Records, 2012.

91 **"Our inability to recall":** Gilbert, *Stumbling on Happiness*, 231–32.

91 **extensive study of more than nineteen thousand:** Jordi Quoidbach et al., "The End of History Illusion," *Science* 339, no. 6115 (January 2013), https://www.science.org/doi/10.1126/ science.1229294.

92 **"Now I feel about sobriety":** McKowen, *We Are the Luckiest*, 117.

5 THIS WILL NEVER STOP BEING YOUR THING UNTIL YOU FACE IT.

105 **"All humans are called":** Veronica Valli, interview with Laura McKowen, *Tell Me Something True*, podcast, June 23, 2022, https:// podcasts.apple.com/us/podcast/veronica-valli-on-the-promise-of -emotional-sobriety/.

105 **"In 100 percent of the documented":** Augusten Burroughs, *This Is How* (New York: St. Martin's Press, 2012), 232.

105 **"Having to say":** Caroline Myss, *Entering the Castle* (New York: Atria, 2007), 347.

109 **"a Bigger Boat":** *Jaws*, directed by Steven Spielberg, Universal Pictures, 1975.

110 **tied to our Puritanical roots:** Matthew Hutson, "Still Puritan After All These Years," *The New York Times*, August 3, 2012, https:// www.nytimes.com/2012/08/05/opinion/sunday/are-americans -still-puritan.html.

110 **Add in hyper-individualism:** S. Rufus, "Self-Hatred: Made in America?," *Spirituality and Health*, accessed May 23, 2022, https://www.spiritualityhealth.com/blogs/worthy-a-self-esteem -blog/2016/09/23/anneli-rufus-self-hatred-made-america.

110 **Sharon Salzberg, a world-renowned:** Sharon Salzberg, "Sit," July 28, 2014, https://www.sharonsalzberg.com/sit/.

115 **most powerful, science-backed:** Emma Seppälä, "18 Science- Backed Reasons to Try Loving-Kindness Meditation," *Psychology Today*, September 15, 2014, https://www.psychologytoday.com/us/

blog/feeling-it/201409/18-science-backed-reasons-try-loving -kindness-meditation.

115 **feelings of social connection:** Bethany E. Kok et al., "How Positive Emotions Build Physical Health: Perceived Positive Social Connections Account for the Upward Spiral Between Positive Emotions and Vagal Tone," *Psychological Science* 24, no. 7 (July 2013): 1123–32, https://doi.org/10.1177/0956797612470827.

115 **increasing positive emotions:** Barbara L. Fredrickson et al., "Open Hearts Build Lives: Positive Emotions, Induced Through Loving-Kindness Meditation, Build Consequential Personal Resources," *Journal of Personality and Social Psychology* 95, no. 5 (November 2008): 1045–62, https://doi.org/10.1037/a0013262.

116 **activating empathy:** Olga M. Klimeki et al., "Functional Neural Plasticity and Associated Changes in Positive Affect After Compassion Training," *Cerebral Cortex* 23, no. 7 (July 2013): 1552–61, https://doi.org/10.1093/cercor/bhs142.

116 **"Mindfulness enables us":** "Loving-Kindness Meditation with Sharon Salzberg," *Mindful,* October 8, 2020, https://www.mindful .org/loving-kindness-meditation-with-sharon-salzberg/.

119 **"[This generation] has lost":** Cal Newport, *Digital Minimalism* (New York: Portfolio/Penguin, 2019), 136.

119 **spending intentional time alone:** Esther Bucholz, "The Call of Solitude," *Psychology Today,* updated June 9, 2016, https://www .psychologytoday.com/us/articles/199801/the-call-solitude.

121 **"tiny, tiny little control issues":** KJ Dell'Antonia, "Anne Lamott Answers Your Questions," *The New York Times,* April 19, 2012, https://archive.nytimes.com/parenting.blogs.nytimes .com/2012/04/19/anne-lamott-answers-your-questions/.

122 **While the prayer was made famous:** "Origin of the Serenity Prayer: A Historical Paper," Alcoholics Anonymous, https://www .aa.org/sites/default/files/literature/assets/smf-129_en.pdf.

123 **one of the many cognitive distortions:** Katherine Compitus, "12 Radical Acceptance Worksheets for Your DBT Sessions," *Positive Psychology,* October 20, 2020, https://positivepsychology.com/ radical-acceptance-worksheets/.

127 **"When a plane is in integrity":** Martha Beck, *The Way of Integrity* (New York: Open Field, 2021), xiii.

128 **Michael Slepian, a professor at:** Michael Slepian, *The Secret Life of Secrets* (New York: Crown, 2022).

129 **The general guideline is:** Ibid.

130 **research shows that instances:** Ibid.

130 **"Boundaries are clear limits":** Melissa Urban, *The Book of Boundaries* (New York: Dial Press, 2022), 6.

132 **Anger is a natural response:** Karen McLaren, *The Language of Emotions: What Your Feelings Are Trying to Tell You* (Boulder, Colo.: Sounds True, 2010), 167–78.

133 **Next, ask yourself the following:** These inquiry questions were adapted directly from McLaren, *Language of Emotions,* 167.

136 **understand our experience exactly:** McKowen, *We Are the Luckiest,* 101.

140 **remains "top down":** Van der Kolk, *The Body Keeps the Score,* 3.

140 **"bottom up" approaches:** Ibid., 3.

6 YOU CAN'T DO IT ALONE.

145 **now often pathologized:** Maia Szalavitz, "Codependency Is a Toxic Myth in Addiction Recovery," *The New York Times,* July 8, 2022, https://www.nytimes.com/2022/07/08/opinion/codependency-addiction-recovery.html.

147 **"Without the understanding":** David Whyte, *Consolations* (Langley, Wash.: Many Rivers Press, 2015), 84.

147 **"Falling upward is a secret":** Richard Rohr, *Falling Upward* (San Francisco: Josey-Bass, 2011), xxvi.

149 **shame is highly correlated:** Brené Brown, "Listening to Shame," filmed March 2012, TED Talks, 20:37, https://www.ted.com/talks/brene_brown_listening_to_shame.

149 **shame can't survive in:** Ibid.

158 **"When the student is ready":** The original source of this quote is unknown, but it is commonly attributed to the Buddha Siddhartha Gautama.

160 **"the crab effect":** Loretta G. Breuning, "When Others Hold You Back," *Psychology Today,* March 6, 2019, https://www.psychologytoday.com/us/blog/your-neurochemical-self/201903/when-others-hold-you-back.

7 ONLY YOU CAN DO IT.

177 **"The word 'dharma'":** Stephen Cope, *The Great Work of Your Life* (New York: Bantam, 2012), 21.

178 **"our unique blueprint":** Ibid.

178 **"Every man has a vocation":** Thomas Merton, *No Man Is an Island* (New York: Houghton Mifflin Harcourt, 2002), 157.

179 *We can only become ourselves:* Ibid., author's paraphrase.

183 **classic folktale from:** The original source of this tale is unknown,

but it is commonly attributed to Martin Buber's book *Tales of the Hasidim* (New York: Shocken Books, 1961).

8 YOU ARE LOVED.

190 **"I do not understand the mystery":** Anne Lamott, *Traveling Mercies* (New York: Anchor, 2000), 143.

195 **"The curious paradox is":** Carl Rogers, *On Becoming a Person* (New York: Mariner Books, 2012), 17.

199 **"If you really want to motivate":** Kristin Neff, *Self-Compassion* (New York: William Morrow, 2011), 167.

201 *"come with your swollen heart":* Warsan Shire, "first thought after seeing you smile," unknown.

9 WE WILL NEVER STOP REMINDING YOU OF THESE THINGS.

213 **"If you could imagine the most incredible story ever":** John O'Donohue, "The Question Holds the Lantern," *The Sun,* https://thesunmagazine.org/issues/407/the-question-holds-the-lantern.

RESOURCES

BOOKS ON ADDICTION

Edwards, Griffith. *Alcohol: The World's Favorite Drug*. New York: Thomas Dunne, 2002.

Grisel, Judith. *Never Enough: The Neuroscience and Experience of Addiction*. New York: Doubleday, 2019.

Lembke, Anna. *Dopamine Nation: Finding the Balance in the Age of Indulgence*. New York: Dutton, 2021.

Szalavitz, Maia. *Unbroken Brain: A Revolutionary New Way of Understanding Addiction*. New York: St. Martin's Press, 2017.

BOOKS ON BOUNDARIES

Tawwab, Nedra Glover. *Set Boundaries, Find Peace: A Guide to Becoming Yourself*. New York: Penguin, 2021.

Urban, Melissa. *The Book of Boundaries*. New York: Dial Press, 2022.

BOOKS ON MINDSET, MINDFULNESS, AND SELF-COMPASSION

Dweck, Carol. *Mindset: The New Psychology of Success*. New York: Ballantine, 2016.

Neff, Kristin, *Self-Compassion: The Proven Power of Being Kind to Yourself*. New York: William Morrow, 2015.

Tolle, Eckhart. *The Power of Now*. Novato, Calif.: New World Library, 1999.

BOOKS ON SOBRIETY

Grace, Annie. *This Naked Mind: Control Alcohol, Find Freedom, Rediscover Happiness, and Change Your Life*. New York: Avery, 2018.

Gray, Catherine. *The Unexpected Joy of Being Sober*. London: Aster, 2017.

Hepola, Sarah. *Blackout: Remembering the Things I Drank to Forget*. New York: Grand Central Publishing, 2015.

Johnson, Anne Dowsett. *Drink: The Intimate Relationship Between Women and Alcohol*. New York: HarperWave, 2014.

Knapp, Caroline. *Drinking: A Love Story*. New York: Bantam Dell, 2005.

McKowen, Laura. *We Are the Luckiest: The Surprising Magic of a Sober Life*. Novato, Calif.: New World Library, 2020.

Warrington, Ruby. *Sober Curious: The Blissful Sleep, Greater Focus, Limitless Presence, and Deep Connection Awaiting Us All on the Other Side of Alcohol*. New York: Harper One, 2018.

Whitaker, Holly. *Quit Like a Woman: The Radical Choice to Not Drink in a Culture Obsessed with Alcohol.* New York: Dial Press, 2019.

White, Amanda E. *Not Drinking Tonight: A Guide to Creating a Sober Life You Love.* New York: Hachette, 2022.

Valli, Veronica. *Soberful: Uncover a Sustainable, Fulfilling Life Free of Alcohol.* Boulder, Colo.: Sounds True, 2022.

BOOKS ON THE RELATIONSHIP BETWEEN TRAUMA AND ADDICTION

Levine, Peter. *Waking the Tiger: Healing Trauma.* Berkeley, Calif.: North Atlantic Books, 1997.

Maté, Gabor. *In the Realm of Hungry Ghosts: Close Encounters with Addiction.* Berkeley, Calif.: North Atlantic Books, 2010.

Van der Kolk, Bessel. *The Body Keeps the Score: Brain, Mind, and Body in the Healing of Trauma.* New York: Penguin, 2014.

RECOVERY PROGRAMS AND COMMUNITIES

Alcoholics Anonymous
Monument
Recovery Dharma
Refuge Recovery
SMART Recovery
The Luckiest Club
This Naked Mind
Women for Sobriety

SOBRIETY COMMUNITY INSTAGRAM ACCOUNTS

asobergirlguide
joinclubsoda
joinmonument
reframe_app
sans_bar
sherecovers
soberblackgirlsclub
soberbrowngirls
sobergirlsociety
sobermomsquad
sober.powered
sobervoices
theluckiestclub
thisnakedmind
1000hoursdry

SOBRIETY PODCASTS

Champagne Problems
Hello Someday
HOME Podcast
In Recovery
Recovery Happy Hour
Recovery Rocks
Seltzer Squad
Sober Curious
Sober Powered
This Naked Mind

PHOTO: KIM INDRESANO

LAURA MCKOWEN is the author of the bestselling memoir *We Are the Luckiest: The Surprising Magic of a Sober Life*. In 2020, she founded The Luckiest Club, a global sobriety support community, and she also hosts the *Tell Me Something True* podcast. She lives with her daughter and her partner in Boston.

ABOUT THE TYPE

This book was set in Baskerville, a typeface designed by John Baskerville (1706–75), an amateur printer and typefounder, and cut for him by John Handy in 1750. The type became popular again when the Lanston Monotype Corporation of London revived the classic roman face in 1923. The Mergenthaler Linotype Company in England and the United States cut a version of Baskerville in 1931, making it one of the most widely used typefaces today.